Mouse Trap
Memoir of a Disneyland Cast Member

by Kevin Yee

Mouse Trap
Memoir of a Disneyland Cast Member

by Kevin Yee

Ultimate Orlando Press
Orlando, Florida

Mouse Trap: Memoir of a Disneyland Cast Member
by Kevin Yee

Published by
ULTIMATE ORLANDO PRESS
www.ultimateorlando.com

Cover design by "The Dozak"

This book makes reference to various Disney copyrighted characters, trademarks, marks, and registered marks owned by The Walt Disney Company and Disney Enterprises, Inc.

Mouse Trap is not endorsed by, sponsored by, or connected with The Walt Disney Company and/or Disney Enterprises, Inc. in any way.

ISBN-10: 0-9773758-1-1
ISBN-13: 978-0-9773758-1-3
Library of Congress Control Number: 2008901893

FIRST EDITION
Printed in the United States of America

For my father.

These may be my memories and my words, but many of them might have faded into the mists of time were it not for the help of my fellow Café Orleans crewmates Stan, Steve, Rudy, Hank, and Dawson, who helped with many of the facts and stories in this book. Thanks are due to Eric Main, Jason Schultz, and Sean Wilson for their edits early on. Marty Klein also provided numerous fixes, and Steve Bauer unleashed a humbling torrent of corrections and editorial suggestions that dramatically improved readability. I am severely in his debt.

My wife Michelle and sons Devon and Tyler deserve special recognition for their patience and forbearance during the creation of this book.

This book is dedicated to the memory of my father, who was supportive of my Disney habit, even if he didn't fully understand it. He also sensed early on that my future lay at least partly in writing. This one's for you, Dad.

INDEX

Introduction

Over the course of fifteen years (1987-2002), I worked a number of jobs at Disneyland. Much of this time was spent in New Orleans Square Restaurants at various locations. I started off in Café Orleans. This restaurant began its existence as a table service location, but when I first worked there, it was in a transitional hybrid state I think of as the "Old Café," and I spent a good deal of time there when it was the "New Café" buffeteria tray slide. A few years after I left, it became the "New New" Café, once again a table service eatery, but I never worked there when it was table service.

I also worked at the Royal Street Veranda, the La Petite Patisserie (commonly called simply the "Pastry Window"), the Blue Bayou, the underground employee-only cafeteria, and the New Orleans Main Kitchen (NOMK), also underground, where much of the prep work was done and dishes and pots were cleaned. I was an hourly manager type for much of this  time—Working Lead, to use the Disney term—and I spent a couple of years being a Lead at the French Market and Mint Julep Bar, too. At the end of my Disney career, I switched into something completely different: I became "crew" or installer for temporary displays and signage around the park, working for a department called Entertainment Art. It was the chance of a lifetime to explore the nooks and crannies of what by then was called the Disneyland Resort, and to get paid while doing it.

But those early years remain the ones which have influenced me the most. Lifelong friendships were forged in those days at the Café Orleans, and my entire outlook on Disney has been colored by those formative years. I learned about the Disney history and company culture at a time when the old ways were still common, and Disneyland was still just a small family. That would change in the coming years, for this was the early phase of Michael Eisner's tenure as Disney's CEO, when he was focused on the studio for a while before turning his attention to the theme parks. In 1987, Disneyland was still functioning as it had for a few decades. In other words, I had just the barest taste of what Disneyland must have been like in the days when Walt Disney roamed the park, and those impressions have guided my sense of what "proper Disney" attitudes, entertainment, service, and show standards should be. It may be that my first year at Disneyland, three years after a crippling strike in 1984, was already beginning the transition away from a feeling of family and toward a more distant corporate mentality, but there were enough vestiges of the old culture and enough old-timers that the closeness was still apparent in many particulars.

I didn't put in quite fifteen years of service, as there was a year or two off between a couple of the jobs listed above, but I always seemed to come back to the park, as though drawn by some invisible force. The source of my fascination can be traced to two factors. First, lightning struck in the mix of people and personalities at the Café Orleans. It's just not that common any more that an entire crew of folks would stay at Disneyland for years at a time, but a large circle of my friends and I did just that, and at least part of the reason is that we didn't want to leave each other, as corny as that sounds. We were having too much fun. Second, the entire Disney experience and the wider Disneyland community-as-family resonated with my sensibilities and struck a chord deep within me. In short, I felt like I belonged at Disneyland. There's no other reasonable explanation why working for an amusement park could seem to me to be so unspeakably cool, even when it's not one of the glamour jobs at the high-profile attractions. After all, it's just a carnival with lots of details and theming, right?

Well, no, it's not. Disneyland is much more than a carnival, or an amusement park, or even a theme park. It's more than the sum of its parts. It's a cultural touchstone, a piece of Americana, and an integral part of our national character. In a little less than a hundred acres, Disneyland captures and encapsulates much of our country's history and all of our recent cultural movements. The "lands" of Disneyland function like a prism, refracting American public consciousness and character into its constituent parts: here on display is our optimistic vision of the future, our predilection for play and escapism, our nostalgia for childhood and neighborhood roots, our adventurous quest for the exotic, and our desire to explore and conquer nature as our pioneering forebears had done. Disneyland may have started out as Walt Disney's vision, but it has become inseparable from the American dream. Disneyland *is* America, and it was hard not to get caught up in that.

The reality of a workday job at Disneyland is far more mundane, of course. Disneyland works its magic on patrons and employees alike in invisible ways, and all too often we simply know that we *like* it here and can't say why. But I can put my finger on at least a few of the reasons why I liked working at Disneyland, most of which revolve around the older parts of the company culture and the sense of community. It's a formula that for decades kept employees happily investing their entire working lives in Walt's vision. Disneyland is a mouse trap, all right, but it's a gilded cage and one that people for years chose voluntarily. The following is my story, and although some of it is comprised of unrelated events and anecdotes, taken together they paint a picture of the Disneyland experience and help explain why I have chosen to allow Disney theme parks to be my mouse trap.

Welcome to the Disneyland Cast!

It started with a long-planned trip to Disneyland at the end of my junior year of high school, intended as a reward after a punishing year of Honors and Advanced Placement classes. My friends and I stopped for lunch at the Village Haus, where to my surprise the person working the cash register was fellow classmate Cindi.[1] She was the first person I had ever seen working at Disneyland who was someone I had known previously. It simply had not occurred to my 17-year-old mind that one could actually *work* at the Happiest Place on Earth. It was a fantastic, stupendous job, Cindi assured us, and that very day we applied for jobs. One of my friends would eventually be turned down at the last cut to be a costumed character, but the other one ended up at Tomorrowland Terrace, flipping burgers and burning his fingers on every last patty. He didn't last long.

My interview was held with two other interviewees in a small room at the only administration building. Cindi had told us to find the application forms at this same location, just off Harbor Blvd. before the patron entrance to the parking lot. I came back a couple of days later for this group interview. The group format, needless to say, was disconcerting. In retrospect, they were obviously seeking to gauge our comfort level in front of strangers—really a smart way to simulate the theme park environment. As the interviewer asked questions of the three of us, he became interested first in Jack, asking him to stay after the interview for a few one-on-one questions. After that point, he ignored Jack. Eventually he asked me to stay too, and then told the third person they would be in contact.

---

[1] The names of every person appearing in this book, save my own, have been changed.

It turned out he offered a job right there on the spot to Jack and me, at the Café Orleans. Neither Jack nor I had heard of it, but when he mentioned it was the outdoor restaurant in New Orleans Square, we both thought we knew what he was talking about. Later it was obvious we were each thinking of the French Market. Apparently both of our families opted for fast food during the annual visit to Disneyland, and since the Café Orleans didn't fit this description, this location was new to both of us.

Orientation, an all-day affair, would be that next Friday. We were to dress up in slacks and a tie, and Disney would provide the rest. My memory of the day is dominated by the slideshow presentation that spanned multiple screens and used several slide projectors. Mostly we saw images of the Disneyland workers, happily assisting patrons and "making magic." It really worked on my pliable, malleable young mind; I was getting more and more excited to be here. That made me highly receptive to the ideas presented at the Orientation, which, in addition to the usual paperwork, included brochures that introduced the realities of the job through the lens of patented Disney positivism. Thus, it was actively exciting to hear them declare such policies as: "We work while others play" or the rain policy (we had to call our schedulers if it's raining or threatening rain—if we showed up but failed to call, they did not have to pay us the four hours of "report pay").

I bought into the indoctrination whole-hog. No cynicism here! I couldn't wait to get started making magical memories for visiting families. I re-read those Orientation brochures over and over in the weeks ahead and really internalized the philosophy behind the words. In this fashion, I came to know the company culture. For instance, there was an ordering of priorities in the theme park, reduced to simple categories so every worker could remember:

The Four Keys To Our Success
1. Safety
2. Courtesy
3. Show
4. Capacity

In later years, "Capacity" was renamed "Efficiency," but one can see the bias toward attractions in the older naming scheme. I memorized the Four Keys as fervently as mathematical orders of operations, atomic weights of various chemicals, or anything else I was asked to learn at school. At Orientation, they explained how the Keys work: they were always to be seen in a hierarchy, and they had to come in that order. Show should never trump courtesy, for example, and efficiency would have to come last, after ensuring the safety of everyone, courtesy to the visitors, and keeping up the Disneyland "show."

The idea of Disneyland as a "show" permeates every aspect of the working culture. An entire vocabulary was invented and enforced: park visitors are stubbornly referred to only as Guests (never customers), and the workers are Cast Members putting on a Show. Accordingly, any time a Guest can see something, that area is considered On Stage, and the worker-only areas are called Backstage. We don't go to the bathroom On Stage with the Guests; we have our own restrooms Backstage. Similarly, we don't eat, drink, or smoke On Stage. Cast Members don't wear uniforms, they wear Costumes. Even the hiring department I had visited for my interview was called Casting.

As indoctrination, perhaps even brainwashing, the Four Keys were so successful I never forgot them, and they really did become the cornerstone of all action I took as a Cast Member. This is significant because the Four Keys, properly applied, have real ramifications. If efficiency is to take a backseat to Show, then one could try to maximize profit only to the extent that the Show does not suffer. The instant the Show suffers, even a little bit, the integrity of the Four Keys is compromised. Of course, sometimes the Keys work in concert with each other. Operating an attraction so efficiently that the line moves fast is in keeping with the appropriate Show, as well as maximizing the Courtesy Key. After all, a fast-moving line constitutes good Guest service. But dangers lurk. Moving the line so fast that one barks out orders to the Guests arguably crosses the line for the Courtesy Key. Even as a teenager, I was quick to understand there was more to this Disneyland job than met the eye. One would have to exercise judgment all the time.

Cast Members who fully accepted the Disney philosophy into their lives quickly discovered that it seeped pretty deeply into their consciousness, even when they were off the clock. For instance, we were told at Orientation that pointing with one finger is considered rude by many cultures, so we were told to point with either two fingers or the whole hand, fingers outstretched. In short order, I found myself utterly unable to point with one finger, even when out of costume and far from Disneyland. I still point with two fingers to this day.

We learned about the "Disney Look," a set of appearance guidelines that ensured all CMs conformed to the same conservative rules. It wasn't enough to merely look presentable; one also had to look like everyone else, by and large. We were given a booklet that detailed some very specific rules. Earrings were for women only, and only stud earrings were allowed; nothing that dangled or hung down. The earrings could be no larger than a dime. Only one ring was allowed per ear; those with a second earring sometimes tried to cover it up by applying a new adhesive bandage over the second earring every day.

We could wear up to one ring per hand only. There could be no visible tattoos. In 1987, mustaches weren't allowed (that rule would later be relaxed), and facial hair in general was banned. Sideburns had to be kept controlled, and more wild variations were verboten. Equally forbidden were wild haircuts. Certainly nothing could be dyed strange colors, and highlights were not permitted. Step-haircuts were popular at the time, but these were not allowed. In a nutshell, everyone was expected to look 'boring'—that's part of the point of the philosophy, that CMs shouldn't attract attention to themselves. Rather, they should fade into the background and allow the Show to focus on things other than the CM's appearance.

After a boxed lunch, which wasn't particularly tasty but at least was free, we were handed our nametags. These oval badges had a small image of Mickey Mouse at the top, and our first names in big red letters across the middle. Everyone's on a first-name basis here, a tradition going back to Walt's preferences. It helped generate a feeling of family among the Cast, too, and I considered it a valuable lesson in business politics that I was fortunate to learn early.

But our nametags today had something special: a ribbon to be affixed to the nametag proclaiming "We're 32 today!" It turns out the day of my Orientation was coincidentally on Disneyland's birthday, and I later came to cherish July 17 as an important holiday. I think my fascination with

Disneyland history and lore was born right at that moment. I'd never known Disneyland's birthday before, and may not have cared if I had heard it. But because I was a part of it this year, suddenly I took ownership, at least subconsciously, and from that point forward I voraciously devoured any information about Disneyland history.

I should also mention that there is something magical about being handed your nametag. I felt like a Cast Member for the first time, and with a tingle of realization, I knew I was part of the team. Living up to that legacy was presented to us as a challenge, and I eagerly accepted it as such.

We were soon joined at Orientation by Area Tour Representatives. These people, like our hosts until now at Orientation, were regular hourly Cast Members from around the park. Once a week or so, they had a special shift where their job would be to welcome new folks like us, but they'd wear their normal Costumes for the day, so we were surrounded by people in the Canoes, Plaza Inn, Matterhorn, or Small World Costumes. The Area Tour Reps took us away in groups divided up by land; Jack and I went off with folks who would be working in Critter Country, New Orleans Square, Frontierland, and Adventureland. Our Rep explained that the first part of the day was the "pixie dust," but his task was to give an accurate picture of the nuts and bolts of the job.

We saw more realities of the work while on this tour of the area, and the primary outcome of the tour was that we were taken, one at a time, to our departmental offices and introduced to our supervisors. Also, we met

our schedulers, and we were given an initial two-week

training schedule right there on the spot. In those days, schedules for two weeks at a time were handwritten in pencil and posted outside the office, up to two sets at a time (the current two-week schedule and the next one). Thus, there was one magical day every fourteen days when you'd know your schedule for the next month, and you'd always know at least two weeks' worth of schedules.

Back at the administration building, we were shown a video of what to expect on our first day of regular work. We'd park in the employee lot, having been given a Cast Member (CM) parking sticker at this Orientation. Then we'd walk to the guard shack marking the start of the Backstage, called Harbor House, so named because it was close to Harbor Blvd. There we would show our hire-in paperwork and government ID, and punch the time clock with our paper timecard. In future visits, we'd have our ID cards, but that was something to get on this first day. We'd have to navigate the lockers ourselves and get our own Costume issued by Costuming, and then get dressed and report to work. We'd go to Security and show our hire-in paperwork, and they would take our photos and issue us the Disneyland ID card. We would need to flash this to get past Harbor House in the future. My first summer, these cards were just colored cards, with no barcodes and no magnetic strips. They were laminated by job type: seasonal workers got red cards, and everyone else got yellow, except for salaried managers, who had blue. In 1988, a newer version with a barcode was implemented, and then in the mid-90s a still newer version with both barcode and magnetic strip was put into production.

On Orientation day, we were shown two videos to illustrate everything we'd have to do on that first day of work with the costume and the ID card. The first video showcased a bumbler who got nothing right and was late to work that first day, while the other video showed a new hire who did everything picture-perfect. In later days, new hires were met when they crossed into Backstage, and an experienced CM trainer walked them through everything. But we were merely shown a video and asked to do it all ourselves. On my real first day, I managed to do everything right and not be late, though I did have trouble dressing myself in the costume. It came with a clip-on bowtie, which took some doing to figure out, and it always slipped off. Later, someone showed me that bending the metal prongs backwards could tighten them so it didn't slip. I had been issued a brand new bowtie, complete with ends hanging down in the Southern style, and it wasn't until I arrived at the location that I learned everyone in the Café ripped out that sash, and I apparently looked slightly ridiculous. Mortified, I modified my tie right away. In hindsight, I realize I probably just looked green and inexperienced, rather than foolish, and I chalk it up to the nervousness of the first day.

All new hires go through Orientation, regardless of their job type, job classification, or worker status. I was hired as a Casual-Temporary (CT), meaning I was expected to work five days a week during school holidays and summer, but otherwise not at all. Later I would become Casual-Regular (CR), meaning I'd work everything the CTs worked but also every weekend during the school year. At the time, Disneyland also had Regular-Part-Time (RPTs) and Regular-Full-Time (RFTs). RFTs worked exactly 40 hours a week in the usual five-day, eight-hour shift pattern. Meanwhile, RPTs worked five days a week, but not every shift was eight hours, so they worked fewer than forty total. But RPTs were guaranteed more hours than CRs. If the alphabet soup didn't confuse us already, there were parallel names for these statuses: the RFTs were called A-status, the RPTs were B-status, and the CRs were C-status. This would lead to spoken shorthand, such as "So, are you a B yet?" In later years, another layer would come between Cs and Bs, called CR-25. This person would work weekends and all holidays and enough other days in the week to usually work 25 hours per week. CR-25s and all Bs and As received health benefits, so when CR-25 was cancelled still more years down the line, some people were upset at the lost benefits.

Apart from health benefits, there were other benefits to being a CM. Chief among them was the ability to visit Disneyland for free when we weren't working. CTs, who were given a highly visible red ID card, could only do so during the summer. CRs and higher could go year round, either on their days off or after working, if the park was open late enough.

CRs and higher were given a pass to admit their own friends or family to the park, called a Main Gate Pass. In later years, all workers got the Main Gate Pass and there was no longer a 90-day delay before they were issued one. The Main Gate Pass let me sign in three guests at a time on twelve separate days of the year (it would later expand to sixteen days per year). Incidentally, the term "sign in" was initially coined because visiting by myself meant flashing my ID card and literally signing my name to a piece of paper at the turnstile. Later, CM card technology was upgraded and they were scanned, but the term "sign in" remained. In the days before annual passports were well-known or indeed marketed, it was highly unusual to be able to visit the park all the time. As CMs, we heard news that the general public in the pre-Internet days did not know, and the sign-in privilege let us capitalize on the news. For instance, there was one magical day in late summer 1987 when a bad evening storm drove out all the Guests, so that the turnstile count implied an incredible one hundred people in the park during that last hour (11:00 p.m.-midnight). Some friends and I went in to the park and found it eerie; CMs were manning all the rides, but we saw zero visitors. We rode all the attractions in Fantasyland in just a few brief minutes.

Another time, I heard through my supervisors, who attended a morning briefing that relayed parkwide news, that one particular day was to be the final day of operation for the Skyway. As a CM with sign-in privileges, I was able to be there, video camera in hand, to witness history. A small historical event, to be sure, but history nonetheless. This ability to witness history would be repeated for other closures too, like the Carnation Plaza Gardens restaurant and the Space Place restaurant.

Another huge benefit came in the form of discounts inside the park. Food was 20% discounted at all venues, as was merchandise at almost every location. For people who had been at the park for at least three years, the merchandise discount soared to 35%, which was called a B-discount (though it had nothing to do with the A-status or B-status discussed above). There were even discounts outside of Disneyland available to CMs; a discount directory listed all of the local businesses which granted 5%, 10%, or even 20% discounts to CMs, presumably as a way to drive additional business.

After the discussion of these and other benefits, the day of Orientation was over. But it wouldn't be the last time I would again set foot inside this part of the Admin building, which bore the name Disney University. This Orientation class wasn't the only class offered at the University. I would be back here in future years for more professional development.

Studying at the Disney University

Disney took professional development seriously, and the company dedicated a good amount of resources, time, and money to making sure the long-term CMs continued to grow and develop. Several different kinds of classes were offered. These weren't things I could sign up for on my own; Cast Members were invited to go at the request of supervisors. Of course, I could always lobby the supervisor to send me to a desired class, and I did so frequently.

Cash Handling

My first class after Orientation was called Cash Handling, which constituted a necessary extra day of training before one could work as a cashier. Often, people took this class right after Orientation, but in my case, I was given cashier status a couple of months later, so it was a special class. Perhaps for that reason, this one was taught not by University Leaders (the guys who usually do Orientation and other such classes), but by a Working Lead in my own location named Kelvin. It was pretty standard stuff, but I was still pretty "green" in my retail experience, so I found it intriguing. We learned to watch for "quick-change artists" who ask questions and try to exchange smaller bills in rapid fashion to confuse the cashier. We got to see and manhandle a collection of counterfeit bills, which was fascinating, and learned to spot the anti-counterfeit features to know when a bill is real. We were also instructed on checking funds in and out, and how to fill out the paperwork.

Train the Trainer

A few months later I was in a class called Train the Trainer, fittingly enough offered when I became an official trainer of new hires at my location. It was here I learned how to train new CMs effectively (and, perhaps more importantly, what to avoid). During Train the Trainer we saw a video called "The Guest." Though the title sounds like it was a Disney production, in fact it was created by an outside company called Media Partners. The class leader told us each copy cost $800, and could we believe that Disneyland purchased three copies? He was trying to make the point that Disneyland cared so much about the message here that it would invest $2,400 in the betterment of its workforce. The video humorously re-made the point about Guests. It's not Disneyland-specific; it's for any service-industry business. Customers should be treated like guests in the home. Be courteous, even when they misbehave. They might get away with misbehaving, but we workers cannot. The costs of re-acquiring an annoyed ex-customer are much higher than retaining one, even if it means taking on apparently extra cost now (such as minor freebies or discounts). In other words, do what it takes to make them leave happy. The humor came about through the various scenarios: a rude Guest and a polite host, a polite Guest and a rude host, or a rude Guest and a rude host. It really drove home the point that paying customers expect a level of service that exceeds even simple courtesy. Satisfaction with the level of service, particular in an industry with so much competition, is just as important as the product itself to the Guest and affects his decision whether or not to return.

Lead Development

After a few years, I became a Working Lead, an hourly version of manager, and was sent to Lead Development, a highly effective class on motivating workers and striking the right balances. Leads were, after all, stuck between the desires of management above and the needs of the hourly workers below. In many ways, it was also a re-sprinkling of pixie dust on battle-hardened veterans of Disneyland in an attempt to remind them of the important lessons from Orientation. I found it highly useful. I got a good perspective not only on Disney policies in general, but also on the purpose for their existence. And such perspective only came since I took this class after being armed with loads of experience.

Guest Complaints for Leads

There was a special class on Guest complaints, where I got to participate in role-plays on defusing angry Guest situations. I was really bad at it at first, but the class helped me become quite a bit better, and these are some of the lessons that remain with me to this day. Disney saw two opportunities when a Guest voices dissatisfaction: the chance to make that one Guest happy again, and the chance to rectify the situation so that no one else goes away dissatisfied. Guest complaints, in other words, were one of the prime ways the CMs could diagnose how well they are performing in Guest service, and they helped to spotlight areas of improvement. Of course, having no complaints at all would represent the highest possible level of achievement.

It was a workshop class, with an informal lecture-style presentation, followed by group Q&A and exercises. During the lecture sequence, many interesting facts came up that will be very familiar to those with a service background, but something many Leads were unaware of until this course. For example, it is estimated that five percent of customers who are dissatisfied with the product or service ever actually complain. So if an attraction receives five complaints daily, in fact as many as 100 people felt dissatisfied. This makes it imperative that Guest complaints be taken seriously and the problem, if it can be fixed, swiftly resolved.

The method of handling a complaint boiled down to just a few steps:

- Listen to what the Guest says. Really listening is not just pretending to do so. React appropriately.
- Some Guests are simply having a bad day at Disneyland, and Leads just happen to be the most convenient target. Let them yell. It costs us nothing to let them yell at us, and the Guest often feels better once he's had a chance to vent.
- Apologize. Always apologize. In fact, we were trained in the LAST technique: Listen, Apologize, Solve, Thank, with special emphasis on the apology. But we were told to be careful how the apology is phrased. Do not say "I'm sorry that you feel that way" because it sounds patronizing and doesn't address the problem. Instead, say: "I'm sorry that we let you down."
- Arrange to fix the problem, and make sure that the Guest knows you will do so. Frequently, the reason a Guest decides to complain is so that no one else will have to suffer the poor product/service that they did. If they know you will fix it, they feel they have accomplished something and that their dissatisfaction has not been in vain.

Turning what starts out as a Guest complaint into an actual Guest compliment is a real art, but it can be done more often than one might think. A Guest who knows he has been heard, really listened to, and whose advice has been taken, is a happy Guest. Some of my most favorable Guest compliments began life as a Guest complaint.

Body language is crucial. There is no one right answer here. Sometimes a sympathetic smile is called for; at other times I'd want to mirror the Guest's sincerity, avoiding what might be seen as a patronizing happy look. In short, I had to learn to read people.

Above all, be on their side and not against them. This is the crucial non-quantifiable element to a good handling of a Guest complaint. Do not phrase it as an us-vs.-them situation. Avoid the use of negatives (what we cannot do) and instead focus on the positives (what we can offer instead).

People skills help. Strategies include matching my mood to theirs—i.e., down in the dumps and angry—and gradually elevating the mood toward a positive outlook, so that they come with me quite naturally and indeed unconsciously.

Some Guests shout. Loudly, even. By acting counter-intuitively, the situation can be defused rather easily: simply lower my own volume. If I speak softly, the Guest usually softens up his tone—again, naturally and unconsciously.

Be professional. Some Leads had a business-style suit. I was reminded that I should take the time to don the jacket of the suit when heading out to take a Guest complaint. It demonstrates to the Guest that I consider their opinion important enough to stop working and listen to them. It also shows them that I am, indeed, the manager and can effect the kind of change they want.

The class even veered into the more difficult questions, such as: Is the Guest always right? Is there no such thing as the Guest being wrong? Well, the answer is: the Guest can, of course, be wrong, but this should never be said or implicitly acknowledged to the Guest, or even believed in his presence. The guiding principle is to treat all Guests like VIPs. Unfortunately, occasionally this leads some Guests to think they are "more VIP" than other Guests, a proposition that goes against the idea that *all* Guests are VIPs, none more than others. This can cause friction, and handling this kind of complaint is the most tricky. I don't want the Guest to think that I'm telling him he is wrong. The trick is to maneuver him into the mindset I have, but without arguing or contradicting.

Let him "realize" the truth and "win" the argument. This takes practice.

Accordingly, the final part of this very helpful class was some practice. The instructor, or another classmate, played an angry or dissatisfied Guest, and I got to play myself: a hurried and flustered Lead.

I did poorly.

The instructor pointed out that my word choices and phrases could be softened considerably. The phrase "what you need to realize" should never be used. Of course, having done poorly made me all the more aware of the proper way to do it, and this is exactly the way things are supposed to work—you make your mistakes in the classroom and not "out there" where it counts for real.

One of our classmates did very well. The instructor-as-incensed-Guest eventually broke out laughing and couldn't continue because the Lead was so genuinely sweet, considerate, soft-spoken, and sympathetic that it became impossible to still be angry at all, let alone with her. I learned a lot from watching that exchange.

In the years since the class, not only have I not forgotten the lessons, they've actually accumulated and become more firmly lodged in my mind. It's hard for me to witness any sort of customer complaint in any service facility without judging the manager's performance. The cardinal errors seem to be an insincere attitude of just paying "lip service" to the irritated customer so they will go away, or an air about them implying that the manager is busy and has better things to do, so the Guest needs to "hurry up already" with the complaint. A lot of managers in the world could benefit from this course.

Performance Appraisals for Leads
There was even a class dedicated to Writing Performance Appraisals, so that Working Leads could learn how to

effectively evaluate the CMs they work with. The appraisal form was purposefully not called a review, since that term implies only past performance. Stress was given in this class on seeing the form for its true value: future performance, ability, and opportunities for growth. The appraisal was designed to be a tool for improvement, not an instrument of punishment or reward.

Casual-Temporary workers, the kind who only work school holidays, had an abbreviated appraisal form with these categories: "Disney Courtesy," "Appearance," "Attitude," "Attendance," "Working Relationship," and "Adaptability." More permanent Cast Members had several additional categories. "Disney Courtesy" referred to interaction with both Guests and co-workers. "Appearance" was mostly a judgment about adherence to the Disney appearance policy. "Attitude" had to do with general job interest and outlook, "Attendance" referred to absences and punctuality, and "Working Relationship" concerned the CM's ability to integrate into a working culture of varied skills, beliefs, and industriousness. To my mind, one of the most important was the final category, "Adaptability." How willing was the CM to learn new job responsibilities and to be flexible with assignments?

Many of these categories overlapped, particularly attitude and adaptability, and often they moved in lockstep. Someone with poor attendance was more likely to not adhere to appearance guidelines, for example. The CM was graded in each category with these possible results: EXCEEDS Disney standards, MEETS Disney standards, DOES NOT MEET Disney standards, and DISREGARDS Disney standards. This skewed scale (one good, one neutral, and two "bad" grades were possible) resulted in a lot of neutral grades. The fourth grade, disregarding Disney standards, was akin to an "F" in school and was only used for real problem cases, or to signal a very significant "opportunity for growth."

Lastly, there was an area for written comments in prose, which is mostly what this class was about. The actual "grades" were pretty easy to fill in on the chart, since each chart helpfully included a description of each point on the scale. For instance, under "Attitude," the various grades stated:

- Able to inspire coworkers
- Has a genuine interest in improving
- Occasionally shows indifference
- Demonstrates little interest in job performance

Since Leads worked with the CMs on a daily basis, it was fairly easy to judge what a fair grade might be. When it came to the written comments, though, Leads had less of an idea what to say. Leads were frequently college students with one or more years of experience as a non-Lead CM, so they had no real training in this sort of thing, shy of this class.

The seminar included pointing out the basics of writing, and writing in such a way as to anticipate what sorts of questions the CM will have during the review. There were charts of helpful suggestions for adjectives and verbs in the booklet, as well.

THEME PARK OPERATIONS PERFORMANCE APPRAISAL

Name _Kevin Yee_   Department _959_   Location _French Market_
Date _February 1996_   Classification _culinary host_

Levels of Performance:

"CO" -Clearly Outstanding-	Distinguished performance. Consistently surpasses expectations and maintains an exemplary level of performance.
"EE" -Exceeds Expectations-	Consistently performs above expectations with minimal follow-up. Sets an example for others.
"MS" -Meets Disney Standards -	Performs to and sometimes exceeds Disney's high standards.
"BE" -Below Expectations -	Occasionally achieves expected level of performance. Needs frequent monitoring.
"UP" -Unacceptable Performance	Performance needs prompt and sustained improvement. Requires constant follow-up.

PERFORMANCE BEHAVIOR	EXPECTATION	CO	EE	MS	BE	UP
ATTENTION TO SAFETY	Demonstrates concern for guest and Cast Member safety. Follows all proper safety procedures.	X				

One helpful section of the class dealt with the issue of objectivity and subjectivity, for this is most often the area where problems arise. By this I mean that the CM's proper execution of expectations might hinge on the line between objective and subjective reasoning. But it also meant that objective and subjective writing were important for the Leads, when writing the comments. Leads were encouraged to be descriptive, not judgmental. And they were to use facts, not inferences, as the basis of their appraisal.

To make the appraisals easy, we kept a collection of index cards at the location, with each CM having at least one card. Known as Incident Cards or IC cards (the name duplicated itself), they were to be updated whenever CMs did something of note, either positive or negative, and a year's worth of such notes made writing the appraisal easy, though Leads were vastly uneven in how often they updated the IC cards. Even less frequently updated were the D-208 cards. Officially known as supervisor's record cards, they were more often referred to as D-208s, since that was the form number. D-208s were more formal variations on the IC cards, kept permanently, and they were held at the "area office," which for us meant they were held in Adventureland. Usually the D-208s were only updated when serious discipline was meted out, or when someone external to the department caught a

CM misbehaving, such as when CMs used the 20-minute parking lot as a regular parking spot, and got a ticket as a result.

Finally, the class touched on the appraisal meeting itself, when the CM sits down with the Lead to verbally discuss the written appraisal. Such items as the need for privacy, advance notice, and effective listening / interviewing techniques were covered, since Leads might otherwise not think of such "trivialities."

We Create Happiness

The granddaddy of advanced courses for Leads was called We Create Happiness. This program had presentations, group work, and even an operation out in the field On Stage. The idea here was to further educate and develop the Leads into effective, honed, and razor-sharp management machines, capable of motivating teamwork and fostering a Disney-style work atmosphere, the kind that just brims with productive energy and showmanship.

The workshop title, We Create Happiness, dated back to a similarly named program for all Disneyland workers designed by Disney University founder, Van Arsdale France. Walt

Disney created the Disney University in 1955 because he
sensed the people he hired didn't fully understand his vision
and needed to have it explained to them. It has since become a
model in the industry for corporate training. Although the
We Create Happiness class dated back to the beginning, by my
day it was only for Leads, and the title seemed appropriate,
given the role Leads play. The buck stopped there, with the
Leads. The first line of defense, so to speak, the Leads were the
lowest version of management and thus were most in contact
with the Cast Members and their performance. Therefore a
good Lead understood and seamlessly integrated a whole host
of considerations, such as:

- What factors influence the CM's sense of motivation?
- How can we assist the CM in making his job easier?
- How can the CM's job be done more effectively or
  courteously?
- More importantly, how exactly do we go about
  implementing this change?

The key here seemed to be avoidance of top-down
management and simple hierarchy. A Lead should never say
"I'm your boss, so you have to do what I say." That wouldn't
make for a very effective manager, and it certainly wouldn't
make for very motivated workers.

The emphasis instead was on understanding motivations
and using that knowledge to promote teamwork. A series of
miniature lectures and anecdotes really helped drive the point
home, and then we broke into small groups, with instructions
to take a box of unwrapped straws and 8-point connectors,
and build the largest structure we could with them. Within
each group, the members were broken down into assigned
units of leader, observer, and workers.

I noticed that the other groups were all building Towers of
Babel out of straws, and remembering the exact directions, I
murmured to our leader that we should be thinking "outside

the box" here. A bigger overall structure could be built more quickly if simple cubes were constructed next to each other along the ground. Go for area and volume, not height. My instinct proved correct, and we won. But it was a conditional win. I had misunderstood the point, which was relying upon teammates, and as the silent observer, I should not have influenced anything.

Other topics covered by the course included safety issues, sexual harassment, crime, Disney appearance guidelines, and a whole range of things. But the primary thumbnail method of summing up Disney management was the Four Keys: Safety, Courtesy, Show, and Efficiency. We spent quite a bit of time discussing how those Keys interrelated in real-world situations, and it's not as easy as one might think. The push for profitability (efficiency) is so strong that frequently agonizing decisions about sacrificing Show take place. How much disruption of the status quo is considered a breach of Show? And so on.

Afterward came the good stuff. We were dressed that day in our own business casual clothing, not our normal costumes, so we took off our nametags and set out into Disneyland with the directive to observe certain things being done by Cast Members everywhere. Were they pointing correctly? Were they rude or disinterested? Did they seem bored? How efficient were they, and how did they balance Efficiency with Show and Courtesy? How successful were their efforts at balancing them?

After a few hours of this, we met up again to compare notes and discuss what we had observed. Naturally we went over the things done right, and more importantly the reason that they were right. When we got to the things done wrong, we were able to make informed suggestions about how to do them differently, and how to suggest the new changes to the CM.

But it's not just all theory and talk. My partner in the walk and I had headed over to the camera stand along Small World Way, where we were greeted with rudeness, boredom, and inattention. My partner, herself a supervisor and known as "Big Bird" to her hourly crew, decided to take that issue up with the supervisor for Fantasyland Merchandise when our little exercise was over.

In a way, the Disney University was just like a real university, with lower and upper division courses. The employee stores even sold Disney University clothing, including baseball caps that had "DU" embroidered on them. The university courses were designed to re-focus Cast Member attention on the Guests. Too often, lethargy set in after a while at the workplace, and this attempt at re-education combated it fairly well. Besides, since the Leads and Trainers got the special courses, the idea was that their renewed energy and tactics would "trickle down" to the other Cast Members. I adored all these visits back to the Disney University. I learned so much at each new class, and the results were directly transferable back to my place of work.

After a time, I began to make direct connections between my job and the very marketable skills I was learning. It even occurred to me to write a book on the management wisdom imparted by these classes and the experience as a Lead, something along the lines of "Leadership Lessons from a Disneyland Lead." That book may never have materialized in exactly that form, but pieces of it can be found in this volume.

We Are Family

Is it a cliché to say that Disneyland Cast Members were treated like, and as a consequence themselves acted like, one great big extended family? As hackneyed as the phrase doubtless is, it nonetheless really applied to the Disneyland Cast, at least during the early years of my time there. This was partly due to the insistence upon first names as described earlier, but mostly related to the company culture that had persisted for decades. The company had no hesitation in putting on activities and granting perks to its workers, even when that involved spending money on them. As a result, I have scores of memories of such events. Some were done to knit departments together as a unit, while others were created simply to reward people on a regular basis. The idea was to make sustainability possible, to keep people happy so they would continue working at the company for years. By and large, it worked. Here are my recollections of the cast activities I lived through:

Canoe Races
It's one of the highest-profile traditions at Disneyland: teams, usually composed of people from the same department, compete in a tournament to race a canoe around Tom Sawyer Island in the fastest time possible. For weeks, teams woke up at the crack of dawn, parked over by the Indiana Jones Adventure show building, since in those days there was a parking lot next to Disneyland, and entered Backstage through a special gate. We'd cross the train tracks and emerge in New Orleans Square, bleary-eyed since it was so early, and get in our canoe and practice. It was an exercise in extreme temperatures. Because it was early, the air was quite cold. To compensate, people often wore heavy clothing. But the work

in the canoes quickly made one hot—much faster than is true when rowing sedately as a Guest during normal canoe operations—and so clothes would have to come off. And yet, water splashed around quite a bit with the frantic rowing, and that water was ice cold so early in the day.

Paddling the canoes in the early morning was a different beast from the Guest version of canoes. For starters, we traveled in the reverse direction, rowing from the canoe dock toward New Orleans Square. On the day of the race itself, the start (and finish) line was at the river stage. But the direction of travel was only one difference. Unlike the On Stage version of this attraction, there was only one person sitting in each row, so with only half the people, it took more effort to move the canoe forward. Also, there was no CM from the canoes attraction around, meaning we had to handle steering by ourselves. There was a forward and a rear steerer, with the rear person usually also responsible for calling out a tempo: "Stroke! Stroke! Stroke! Switch!" The switch command meant we'd slide from the left side to the right side (or vice versa), and we'd be arranged on the boat in a way that equal numbers would be on both sides at all times. It would only take a couple of minutes to make it around the island—it went much faster than when the canoe was filled with Guests. In fact, it was surprisingly hard work, and reasonably good conditioning. No wonder the guys who worked canoes were always so muscular!

Though we worked hard, we never won. In my day, the men's division was dominated by DC Express, a team composed of guys who worked the canoe ride for a living. So we didn't bother going up against them; we were in the mixed division, with men and women. Our team names were never very inspired, and I don't remember them now. But we did sometimes have inventive names. In the intramural basketball leagues at Disneyland, our team named itself the Jam Session, a riff on the peanut butter and jelly sandwich we served at the Café Orleans, also called the Jam Session. I never played basketball with our team; the canoes were more my speed. While I don't remember our own canoe team name, I do have examples from one year in the early 1990s, when canoe teams included DC Squirrels, High Voltage, Nomad Adventure, Team 1, Rowmen Empire, No More Pins, Lethal Injection, Parking Lot Oars, Beauties and the Beast, Desk Jockeys, Mission Impossible V, Oar Mongers, Splash-n-Crash, Without a Paddle, and PMS (Paddlers of Main Street).

We'd occasionally qualify with the minimum time at the canoe races, but we never made it past the first or second round of the actual tournament play. That's all right; winning might have been nice, but it wasn't the only goal. Invariably, we'd follow up early morning practice with breakfast together at the local Denny's or Spires. The camaraderie was the point.

Disney Family Christmas Party

In early December each year, the company held a Cast Christmas Party. The idea was that employees throughout the Walt Disney Company, including such divisions as the film studio or Walt Disney Imagineering, would be able to enjoy the park as Guests and bring along their family. Since the Disneyland workers were also eligible to attend, there was a need to hold the party on multiple nights to spread out the load of working, and to make sure everyone could have an evening to visit the park.

To make sure Disneyland didn't bear the brunt of filling the shifts alone, folks from the Studio or Imagineering volunteered to fill shifts working at Disneyland for the party on nights when they weren't visiting as Guests. Thus, one could see people from Imagineering pouring sodas or film division advertising executives sweeping up trash at these Cast Christmas parties. These folks got a kick out of doing something different, too—it wasn't just work for them. I could frequently tell who was from the outside, not just because they had a different kind of nametag, but because many of the men sported mustaches. In those days, no facial hair was allowed for Disneyland workers, but there was no such restriction at the studio or Imagineering. That was always jarring to witness.

Monday,
December 4, 1989,
7:00 p.m. to
12 midnight

1989
DISNEY
FAMILY
CHRISTMAS
PARTY

Please bring one new unwrapped toy for Operation Christmas

Present this ticket and your I.D. or Main Gate Pass for admission. This ticket is non-transferable

When I attended the party as a visitor, I had to obtain a special ticket for the evening. In my early years, this was done at Cast Activities, little more than a window. Later, it was done at Company D, a new store for CMs that was originally created to move merchandise that didn't sell out in the park, so it was dramatically reduced in price. In later years, multiple TEAM Centers around the resort were opened to sell merchandise, some of it Cast-specific, and to distribute tickets to events such as these. The first home of Company D was a simple portable trailer like one might see outside a public school, located just outside Harbor House. Later, it moved off-property and became much larger, and arguably lost the sense of family that had characterized its earliest incarnations. Even the name was the result of a contest; regular Cast Members could send in suggestions for the soon-to-be CM overstock store. My suggestion was "Mickey's of Anaheim," a riff on the name of the similar and already-extant store at Walt Disney Imagineering, Mickey's of Glendale (itself inspired by the famous lingerie store Fredrick's of Hollywood).

Visitors arriving at the Family Christmas Party entered through the main turnstiles and saw enormous canisters against the floral Mickey railing; these were for toys being dropped off. CMs were given tickets for all of their dependents (as defined by their tax deductions); or, in some cases, they got one to three tickets to bring along a guest even if they didn't have dependents. Each person through the gate was asked to bring an unwrapped toy for charity worth about $5. All these gifts went to Toys for Tots.

Once inside, we could ride any of the attractions; the park was open for business as usual. This was a real treat for people in the company who didn't normally work at Disneyland, but we Disneylanders could visit rides all year long so the primary interest was seeing the place open with such small crowds! That changed in 1995, though, when Disney acquired CapCities/ABC, and suddenly there were many thousands of new Disney employees. The Family Christmas Party became as crowded as a normal day at Disneyland.

Other things to do during the party included taking a photo at specially set-up locations. There would be a backdrop and a costumed character there to pose with, and every person with a ticket got a Polaroid stuffed into a souvenir sleeve for the event. Then just about everyone headed off to dinner. In my early days, the menu prices were brought down to a level that can only be called "dirt cheap": a dollar for clam chowder in a bread bowl, popcorn for a quarter, and so on. With those prices, the company was barely making back food costs, and not at all paying for labor with the proceeds on the food. Clearly, there was no profit on these nights. But the point was definitely not profit—this party was a celebration for the Cast, as a thank-you for a year of hard work. The feeling of family and community was made all the stronger because the company didn't fleece its workers at the holiday party.

Little Monsters on Main Street

To celebrate Halloween in a fun, safe manner, each year Disneyland opened its doors one evening in October to CMs and their families. Everyone was invited to dress up and do trick-or-treating on Main Street, as though every storefront here was another house to visit, and reap yet more candy. Since the rest of the park wasn't open, the primary attraction was for CMs who had young children.

Backstage Magic

In 1994, we saw the introduction of a new kind of Cast party called Backstage Magic. If there was a catalyst for holding this kind of party besides simply keeping us tightly-knit as a family, I never learned what it was. The entire premise of the party was to invite the whole Disneyland Cast to tour selected Backstage areas to see how Disneyland operated behind the scenes.

The elements that stick out the most include a visit to the Roundhouse, where the Disneyland trains live (and where the monorails live over them, on the second floor), a visit to Circle D Corral, which the horses and ponies call home, and a trip to the Landscaping department, where they took brave visitors on a scary, scary ride up onto a landscaping crane—they called it a hedge trimmer—about a hundred feet up. We were chained in, but the flimsy chain felt absolutely insufficient at those heights!

We were allowed to visit the control rooms of both Space Mountain and Splash Mountain. To accommodate all the visitors despite the rides being open, we were split into small groups and led up to the control room with an escort. Those control rooms are cramped, utilitarian places, and the monitors were much smaller than I'd expected, but it was still fascinating to see close-up.

Another indelible memory came in the form of riding Space Mountain, which was open for the evening, but with all the work lights turned on full blast. This was, after all, a celebration of the Backstage elements of Disneyland. Our ride through the fully-lit mountain was terrifying—one never realizes in the near-dark of the normal operation just how close the coaster cars pass to the girders on the sides, and especially overhead. A few years later, annual passholders were invited to a special party just for them, and they were treated to a completely dark Space Mountain—no show lights or disco ball lights at all. I was an annual passholder by then, so I saw both alternate versions of Space Mountain, and I found the fully-illuminated Backstage one to be the more unusual, and thus the more special.

Cast Blast and Previewing New Attractions

A new concept called Cast Blast was born in 1998. This special party for the Cast may have taken its lead from Backstage Magic a few years earlier, since it didn't fall on a major holiday. But this time, there was an obvious impetus for the soiree: Disneyland was about to unveil "New Tomorrowland 1998," and it seemed only appropriate to let the workers experience the new rides before the general public got to see them. In this, the park was following a long tradition.

From the very beginning, park managers have exposed Disneyland workers to the new rides before the public opening, partly as a way to test the operation in real-world conditions, and partly as a perk for the workers. I got to see Splash Mountain (1989) and Roger Rabbit's Car Toon Spin (1993) under those conditions—the call went out for workers to slip away briefly from their locations, once they had permission of course, and to visit the ride while still in costume. Car Toon Spin had been tested with a teacup on the Roger Rabbit track, to see how the ability to turn yourself around might play out in a real dark ride, but this test was conducted before the Cast got to see it. We saw rides only a few brief days or weeks before the public.

For Splash Mountain, since our restaurants were close by, we visited and tested the ride often, and the process was an extended one, because that project was behind schedule and needed numerous tweaks. Among the problems: a gigantic tunnel of water that surrounded the logs on the final drop—this was visible in the television commercials seen at the time—that made riders so drenched, it had to be changed before the ride could ever be opened to the public. As testers, we got to see the ride in all its drenching glory, and we later took delight in seeing the commercials show the older drop profile, because the real ride that eventually opened up had a much smaller splash.

The show elements were not 100% in place yet. For example, the Br'er Rabbit that laughs as Br'er Bear sticks his nose into bees (and his behind into our faces) was not yet covered by foliage, and his animatronic bottom half was exposed. He's just a half-figure anyway, but this was really obvious. Seeing that during testing drew my attention to it, so I see all its flaws now when I ride, even though it's more hidden. Same thing for the speakers behind the cranes in the Laughing Place—those are better hidden now, but I still notice them because they were even more exposed during testing.

Another thing that's gone now is the song by the mother rabbit to her children (and it was also sung by the mother possum). It changed just before the ride opened—the song nowadays has an ominous tone, which is the whole point of the scene anyway, but the original song was sad. The generic term "Burrow's Lament" could apply to either version of the song. The older one was sung to the tune of "Sooner or Later" and one can still hear an orchestrated version of it in the Critter Country area music (the lyrics included: "sooner or later that rabbit is gonna come home... he's learned his lesson well"). The newer, ominous version is sung to the tune of "Ev'rybody Has a Laughing Place."

Also neat was the way we got to ride during the testing; we'd enter through the back show building, go behind the sets and witness the ugly, unpainted stucco interior, navigate metallic stairways, and end up at the queue near the singing rabbit. Since there was no line, we could cross over the bridge to re-ride if we wanted to. I remember the unpainted interior particularly well. It was made of white stucco, which was very odd to see, since everything at Disneyland is otherwise presented so completely. It really reminded me that these things are sets when viewed from "On Stage."

Fantasmic! was another attraction I was able to see in previews, and it's the one that has been seared most starkly into my memory. By the early 90s, I had become deeply invested in Disneyland's history, and I had read about CMs experiencing wonder when previewing the Tiki Room, so radically new at the time compared to anything that had come before it. Splash Mountain and Roger Rabbit were both good rides, but neither had engendered that kind of slack-jawed stupefaction. Fantasmic! would be that attraction for me. We were invited to pick up tickets for a show after the park had closed one evening, and despite heavy interest from the CMs, there were ridiculous amounts of space still available. That's also stuck in my memory, because it hasn't been true very often since then, so popular is the show with the Guests.

That first viewing marked one of the few times I've ever become so engrossed in a production that I became fully disconnected from my surroundings. The lack of people around me was also the reason, I've concluded after years of thinking about this, why the show seemed so much louder in that preview. The sound just echoed off the walls and buildings and bounced back at me, and the effect was even more spectacular than a normal show of Fantasmic! When the first show ended, my feelings of exultation could not be expressed in words, but I understood for the first time what it must have been like at the Tiki Room in 1963, watching Walt unleash an entirely new kind of entertainment on an unsuspecting world. I beamed, realizing that my job at the Café Orleans (and usual job as the Lead for the closing shift) would mean I'd get to see Fantasmic! all the time, or at least hear it in the background.

Indiana Jones Adventure: Temple of the Forbidden Eye was a different matter altogether. As rough and violent as some people claim that it is now, it was much, much worse when we did the CM testing back in 1995. I loved it! I was blown away by how rough the ride was. It didn't bother me; it made the ride that much more realistic. They toned it down quite a bit before the public ever saw it.

Perhaps the greatest benefit to previewing new rides was psychological. Cast Members felt themselves a part of the Disneyland family when they were invited to try these new offerings out. We felt special, and rightly so. Once the "test and adjust" phase of the attraction was worked out, the ride could be operated in a more consistent "soft opening"—not officially announced as open, and could close at any moment. In those days, the soft openings were done only for the CMs, long before any public operation or the preview event for annual passholders. CMs felt themselves placed at the top of the hierarchy in this fashion, and the early rides themselves became yet another perk, another reward for being part of the team.

While those ride and show tests occurred without much fanfare, there was a more formal affair called Cast Blast that fulfilled some of the same purposes. That first year in 1998 we took a tour of Innoventions, still heavily under construction. Oddly, my main memory is seeing a contraption in there which would be used outside later on: a launcher of soda bottles, to match the theme of rocket take-off at the outdoor vending cart just below the Moonliner rocket. It also sticks in my memory that there was a pin set issued to Cast Members at the time.

Cast Blast in that first year also featured riverboat gambling, mostly blackjack, on the Mark Twain steamboat. This sort of thing was done at Working Lead private parties, but it was always welcome in a general Cast party. That it took place on the Twain lent additional credibility.

One of the defining features of Cast Blast is cast-friendly policies, like completely and utterly free Outdoor Vending (ODV). Free Mickey ice cream and unlimited popcorn made for a festive atmosphere. This tradition stayed alive when Cast Blast moved to Disney's California Adventure (DCA) in that park's first years.

At the other end of an attraction's lifespan, CMs get to bid attractions adieu just before they close. Attractions CMs get the final ride on the closing day and in the final hour. In my years, such rides included the Submarine Voyage and the pre-rehab Autopia.

Working Lead Appreciation Events

Going back as far as I can remember, the special events just for Working Leads around Disneyland have always been there. The first ones I attended, in the late 80s and early 90s, were held at the Disneyland Hotel, in the Grand Ballroom. These were formal affairs, with the participants asked to dress in semi-formal attire, with the entire affair held in lavish circumstances. There was buffet dining available, dancing, two free drinks (and further alcohol for purchase), and faux Vegas-style gambling that used raffle tickets rather than cash. I can recall more than one drunken supervisor who doled out raffle tickets on the basis of popularity rather than gambling winnings, but no one particularly seemed to mind. No one wanted to spoil the mood by pointing out such favoritism. These were fun, celebratory times, and the Lead party was certainly no place to air grievances. Better times simply were not to be had. The Leads in attendance understood that this annual event was meant as a thank-you to them for their yearlong dedication to the park. As the lowest level of management (or rather, the highest level of non-management), Leads really were in that level between a "rock and a hard place," asked to represent management's interests down to the CMs and the CMs' interests up to management. The annual appreciation events reminded the Leads that their efforts, and the sometimes frustrating and difficult positions they found themselves in, were in fact appreciated. My final two Working Lead Appreciation Events were in 1995 (when the theme was Indiana Jones, befitting the 1995 opening of that ride) and in 1996 (when the theme was Mardi Gras). The event was discontinued for a time after 1996, but started again when Disney's California Adventure opened.

Cast Parties

On a smaller scale, regular Cast were invited to department-level parties. To my memory, these did not occur at regular intervals, so they weren't annual affairs, but they seemed to happen every few years. The two big ones I recall involved all of New Orleans Restaurants, a department consisting of several restaurants and more than 500 people, at places like a local park in Anaheim or at Newport Beach.

I recall there being softball and organized games at the park, whereas my memory of the beach event revolves mostly around clam chowder. At these events, we'd self-cater (we were a department of restaurants, after all), and one guy named Matthew was tasked with bringing the chowder down to the beach in the department's pickup truck. Because the truck was usually used just on property, it was always somehow fun and forbidden to take it far away. Matthew brought several pots of chowder with tin foil over the top, but it was all cold and half spilled by the time he arrived. He apologized and explained he'd gotten a flat tire on the 55 Freeway on his way over, which had both spilled a lot of soup and made him late. I think this became lodged in my memory mostly because I could not contemplate the horror of having to change a flat tire on an unfamiliar company truck while racing against the clock to get food to people who were waiting for it. I was stressed just thinking about it. These parties were fun, but it's perhaps a sign of the blandness of them that I don't remember much else.

By contrast, I do have a sharp recall of a French Market-specific party in the years after our department was broken up into smaller business units, but my memory of it is sharp because the experience was so boring it became embarrassing. Our manager had kept down costs by holding the party at the French Market itself, which is fine as far as that goes, but

thought it would be a great idea to have it be a dance party.
Most CMs went to off-property parties all the time, but those
informal affairs were characterized by drinking, not by
dancing. Any dancing that would break out spontaneously
was always alcohol-fueled. Obviously, there was no alcohol at
this party in the French Market, and as a result there wasn't a
lot of dancing, either. I do recall a somewhat fun game of
human bingo, however ("find someone who has rehired three
times," "find someone who has been to Paris," etc.) This game,
like the games at the beach and the city park, did the trick of
reinforcing the idea that the Cast was one big family.

Distinguished Service Award Banquets

When I had worked for Disneyland for a year, I received a
"year pin"—a bronze-colored Steamboat Willie badge that
could be mounted on my nametag in place of the usual image
of Mickey Mouse above my name (in practice, that meant I
was issued a second nametag with no Mickey at all, but a hole
above my name where I could insert the pin). At the five-year
point, there was a Donald pin.

When one got to ten years of service, the recognition
every five years would change to a formal dinner. These were
pretty similar to Lead Appreciation Events and were held at
the Grand Ballroom of the Disneyland Hotel. People dressed
up, there was free food and alcohol, and there was dancing
(but there was no gambling). The special musical guest in the
year that I attended was Jodi Benson, the singer behind Ariel's
songs in the *Little Mermaid*. That the company would bring
out such a star for the rank-and-file CMs really made an
impact on everyone.

On hand was the Cinderella coach used for weddings, so
people could pose with it. An announcer would call up groups
by service year and take a group photo. Everyone celebrating
a particular year (say, the fifteenth year anniversary) would

stand in front of a castle backdrop. The ten-year group photo was big, the fifteen-year smaller, the twenty-year dramatically smaller, and so on. One only got invited to this dinner at five-year intervals, and it only happened once a year, regardless of the time of year one had actually hired in.

Those with ten years of service received a plaque, but those with fifteen or more were given a small statuette in bronze, something pretty similar to what can be seen around the Central Plaza of Disneyland. Each milestone year had its own design; the statue of Walt and Mickey was the pinnacle statue on my visit, representing 45 years of service (Disneyland had not yet celebrated its 50th anniversary when I saw the banquet). It was amazing to think there were a few people in the room who had been there from the beginning, or very near to it. Most of the old-timers worked Backstage, though not all. It was humbling and just a touch awe-inspiring to talk with these folks. Here's the complete list of service awards in 1998 (the pins refer to a small badge to be inserted into a name tag):

1 year	– Steamboat Willie pin
5 years	– Donald Duck pin
10 years	– Castle pin and plaque with Mickey Mouse
15 years	– Sorcerer Mickey pin and castle statuette
20 years	– Mickey pin and watch
25 years	– Tinker Bell-themed pin and statuette
30 years	– Jiminy Cricket-themed pin and statuette
35 years	– Pinocchio-themed pin and statuette
40 years	– Donald Duck-themed pin and statuette
45 years	– Pin and statuette featuring Walt and Mickey together

Group Photos

For Disneyland's 35th Anniversary in 1990, a call went out to get CMs willing to arrive at the crack of dawn one day and pose for a photo, using our bodies and T-shirts given to us, to form a giant "35" logo. I'd seen pictures like these in the past, so I recognized it as a longstanding tradition to take such Cast photos, and I jumped at the chance. I was impressed that the free T-shirt was of heavy-duty quality and sported the 35th logo on its back as well; this was a keeper of a freebie. Taking the photo itself required only a few minutes. The photographer ascended a platform crane, we all waved, and a giant mural of T-shirts was created.

For a time in the early 90s, Disneyland was interested in seeking world records, and the Cast would be invited to be a part of it. For instance, there was the world's largest hula hoop event, with the most people doing the hula hoop at the same time. Called the Super Hooper Duper, it was an idea tied to Disneyland's promotion at the time, Blast to the Past. For similar reasons, Disneyland invited Chubby Checker to the park one morning, before opening to the general public, and had enough Cast Members on hand to break the world record for doing the twist at the same time. Naturally, the real interest was in capturing all of this on video and using it in television spots, to showcase the Blast to the Past theme and lure other folks to Disneyland. No matter; we Cast Members were delighted to be involved in the first place.

Minnie's Moonlit Madness

There had long been an annual "fun run" for Cast Members called the Minnie Marathon, a 5K run through Disneyland in the pre-opening hours. There had also been a road rally throughout Anaheim, using one's own car, called the Great Goofy Pursuit. In 1990, someone came up with the idea to unite the two concepts, and Minnie's Moonlit Madness was born. The trivia-rich, scavenger hunt and puzzle game took place inside Disneyland after hours, with hordes of volunteers there to make the puzzles interactive and social. While the puzzles and checkpoint concepts had similarities to a road rally, albeit one on foot, the constant walking easily added up to five kilometers and often surpassed the distance people had run for the Minnie Marathon. Teams of four originally had to be all CMs, later changed so that only two of the four were required to be. All four were bound together by bungee cords at the hip, ensuring that teams stayed together.

The exact event varied from year to year, but it usually began with a trivia packet and graduated to the puzzle/quest combinations, which were solved one at a time. This usually involved deciphering a word or visual puzzle, which would then ask a question that could only be answered by walking (always speed walking, never running) over to a new location, say the very end of Critter Country, and examining some detail on the walls. Sometimes we were asked to find a special kind of person there—enter that army of volunteers, who would toy with us, act coy, and always stay in character. They seemed to revel in delaying us as much as possible, yet teams always wanted to go faster, get the answer, and move on to the next quest. Once we finally had our final answer, we'd scrawl it on the envelope provided and head back to the Central Plaza, where tables ringed the hub, each table serving its own set of teams. We found the table with our team number on it, exchanged the envelope for a new one, and off we ran again.

As the event gained in popularity and complexity, changes came over it. Chief among them was the difficulty level of the quests. To help teams self-diagnose how to play the game, designers made up ticket books: A-ticket quests were easy, but worth fewer points; E-ticket quests were quite hard, took longer, but were worth more points. To win the game, one no longer needed to be the fastest (and to solve everything correctly), one also had to guess correctly what the right mixture of tickets was. No team could possibly complete five E-tickets, so we just had to guess at a mixture of ticket types that could lead to victory. Getting lucky also helped: not every C-ticket (or whichever level) quest was equally difficult. The coup de grace was that our ticket decision had to be made when we applied for the game, weeks in advance. That way, our exact tickets would be waiting for us when the game began, already at our table. There was no flexibility on the night of the event.

Needless to say, this event was enormously fun. Its token entry fee—$40 per team in those early years—went entirely to charity. They also sponsored a "penny drive" as the event geared up at the start of the night. People brought in giant pouches of pennies, and we saw one guy with a wheelbarrow literally full of pennies, in an effort to help his team bring the most pennies. All of this money also went to charity.

They didn't really encourage people to dress up, but we came up with the idea ourselves. My first year, I played with three other Asian CMs, so we decided to name ourselves the Orient Express. We did quite well! I'm sure it had nothing to do with the fact that we took our pale blue chef bandanas (part of our issued costumes) and tied them around our foreheads like Hollywood samurais. This level of costuming was nothing, however, compared with what came later. As part of a different team, I dressed up in a DEVO T-shirt, as did another member. We donned those recognizable DEVO hats, which looked like pyramids of circles. The final two members of our team also had the hats, but instead of T-shirts they wore yellow powder suits also emblazoned with DEVO on them. We were about as "geeked out" as we could be. Even in the early 90s, DEVO as a band was as much joke as serious music to some people. As we ran through the event, our leader Rupert (this whole DEVO thing was his idea, not mine) shouted as loudly as he could "Are we not men?" to which the three of us shouted back "We are DEVO!" It was meant to be obnoxious but also fun, and after I got over the embarrassment of it all, I started to appreciate the attention. People around us would also shout back "We are DEVO" by the end of the night; I guess our enthusiasm was infectious. It came as little surprise, then, when in future years we saw both pictures and video of our team from that night, cut into montages and photo galleries they would show when advertising Minnie's Moonlit Madness to future players.

I'm proud to say I once placed fourth in the event. I always regretted that this was the closest I ever got to winning a prize, but we were proud to get this close. After CapCities/ABC joined Disney in the mid-90s, the event got larger and larger, and it became ever harder to win.

Name This Location
To add to the feeling that Cast Members were valued members of the family, park managers routinely asked for our help in naming new locations, often holding a contest. I recall a parkwide contest to name the new concept for Company D, the store that sold park merchandise to CMs at a radical discount. More local to my area was a contest to rename the Disneyland Employee Cafeteria (D.E.C.) when it was given a freshened look. Whereas before it was ostensibly a French

café (trust me, this theme was not well expressed), it became more of a 50s diner under the new theme. The winning name, Westside Diner, captured it about right. To this day I have a hard time picturing this same eatery as the Racing Pit, its original theme and name. Old-timers told me it was often shortened to just "the Pit," which was also fitting since this restaurant is underground, below Pirates of the Caribbean.

I can recall taking part in only one naming contest, for the new food location being built next to Splash Mountain. My friends Dale and Dawson suggested "Dale and Dawson" as a name, and I think they seriously submitted that. I took a different tack. Knowing that Splash Mountain was going to be themed after the movie *Song of the South*, I suggested "Br'er Frog's Fishin' Shack," which I thought would fit the theme quite well. In retrospect, that doesn't sound very appetizing, almost like folks would be served frogs' legs. The eventual winner, Harbour Galley, did sound more appealing, if a bit less appropriately themed.

Another thing done to make the CMs feel special was that they got first crack at restaurants, not just rides. This was a sound business practice, because then the front-line folks were well aware of what the new menu had to offer, and could more accurately give advice to Guests, since questions about menus at nearby locations were inevitable and frequent. Wisely, managers kept the prices quite low for these preview days for CMs, so that people would be enticed to eat there. Here was the Cast preview menu for the Harbour Galley in 1989:

- Shrimp Cocktail - $2.40
  A spicy shrimp cocktail with celery and pineapple tidbits
- Cajun Popcorn Shrimp - $2.45

> *A lively Cajun seasoned dish of deep-fried crayfish
> and shrimp with Louisiana-spiced cucumber sauce*

- Seafaring Potato Skins - $1.95
  > *Deep-fried potato skins stuffed with a zesty cheese,
  > shrimp and seafood mixture*
- The Columbia Halibut Sandwich - $3.50
  > *Broiled, tender halibut filet on a honey-wheat bun
  > with mild cucumber sauce, served with seasoned
  > curly fries*
- Land and Sea Fare - $2.75
  > *Chilled smoked albacore, sharp cheddar cheese and
  > apple slices with mild cucumber sauce*
- Admiral Fowler's Fresh Seafood Brochette - $3.95
  > *Succulent, seasoned chunks of fresh fish on a skewer
  > nestled between fresh mushrooms, onions and
  > peppers*
- Clam Chowder in the Harbour - $1.75
  > *Creamy white clam chowder surrounded by a
  > sourdough bread bowl, topped with a pat of butter
  > and a sprinkle of parsley*

Sorcerer's Apprentice

One contest that really stirred the imagination, held only once in 1991, was called Sorcerer's Apprentice and was nothing less than an open call for ideas for new rides from the people who worked at Disneyland. This was thrilling! Suddenly, working at Disneyland was everything I'd imagined as a child. I could finally be a part of designing the magic!

The rules were simple: invent a new ride for Disneyland, and include as much detail as possible. Especially welcome were sketches and diagrams—it was clear they wanted people with artistic talent. Whatever I suggested became the property of Walt Disney Imagineering (WDI); I could not sue years later, claiming that my idea was used without payment. The winner would be offered a permanent job at WDI—a dream come true for a lot of us park workers.

Entranced, I scoured the park, looking for areas that needed refreshing. The Country Bears were looking a little worn, I thought, and I strongly considered a dark ride for the area. In this, I was prescient, for the Many Adventures of Winnie the Pooh would later do just that. But my idea at the time was to capitalize on the then-popular Rescue Rangers. I think I was wise not to pursue this one beyond the thought experiment.

What I did propose was a Disneyland Maglev (magnetically-levitated) train, which would run atop the existing Tomorrowland buildings and out into the lagoon/Autopia area. I had recently heard of tentative plans to rejuvenate Tomorrowland with a theme of "Tomorrowland 2055"—still more futurism but infused with an invasion by whimsical aliens. One highlight would be Plectu's Fantastic Galactic Revue, a musical animatronic stage show put on by aliens in the then-unused America Sings building. The entire Tomorrowland 2055 concept never made it off the drawing board, obviously, but vestiges remain in WDW's Tomorrowland, where an invasion by cute and friendly aliens did make it into reality.

Knowing about the Tomorrowland 2055 proposal, I injected as much of it as I could into my idea for a Disneyland Maglev. But mostly I wasn't thinking about theme as much as I was thinking about expanding Walt's 1960s vision for Tomorrowland as a "World on the Move." There were kinetics aplenty in Tomorrowland in those days, and I envisioned adding still more. Although the land already had two layers, with the PeopleMover and Monorail forming the second layer, I envisioned a third layer atop that, highlighted by the maglev, a "new generation" monorail that runs efficiently by using magnets to avoid all friction.

I'm the first to admit that my proposal wasn't very well presented. Though I did my best with some pencil sketches of the interior, I have no artistic ability to speak of. It came as little surprise that I didn't win. The guy who did win the grand prize, a fellow named David Durham, proposed a little jeep ride in Adventureland. His vision melded nicely with other plans for the area; at one time, there was meant to be a jeep ride and an Indiana Jones themed mine car ride overlapping each other (with intertwined tracks from the Jungle Cruise and the Disneyland Railroad, too). As promised, he was offered a job at WDI and eventually programmed the jeeps at the Indiana Jones Adventure. Besides Durham, five other CMs were offered jobs at WDI.

Spirit Award Pins and Perfect Attendance

The "year pins," mentioned earlier, could be affixed to the top of one's nametag, but these weren't the only kind of pins around. More coveted was the Spirit Award Pin. To win a Spirit Award, one had to be nominated by someone else, and then a committee in that department looked at the nominations and decided who actually deserved the Award. The qualities sought were in keeping with Walt's vision for customer friendliness, which was seen as more important than service to the company.

In my early years, the Spirit Pin was a simple Mickey Mouse shape of three circles, done entirely in elegant silver with no other decoration or drawing. Later, that would change to a silver-colored castle design, which was less recognizable at a distance.

The mere existence of the Spirit Award was enough to spur folks to keep customer service foremost in their minds. If one hoped to win a Spirit Award one day, one was always on one's best behavior and went that extra mile for every Guest that one encountered. At an institutional level, it's a great idea. For a very small outlay of money, the company gets a greatly strengthened adherence to one of its core principles.

A similar principle was employed to encourage perfect attendance among the Cast. Someone with no call-ins at all and who was not late for a whole year earned a plastic license plate frame that wasn't sold and could only be earned in this fashion. It read: "The magic works / and I'm making it happen!" CMs proudly installed it on their cars as something of a status symbol, since all CMs parked in one parking lot and this was one way to "be seen."

Of course, nothing is foolproof. One year my friend Rudy was duly informed of his perfect attendance, but just two weeks later, at his annual performance evaluation, he received a mere "meets expectations" for attendance. What does it take, he wondered, to "exceed expectations"? Or to "far exceed expectations"? He had perfect attendance, after all. While his evaluation was fixed easily enough once he complained, it exposed a flaw in the system. Human foibles were the weak link. Managers tended to evaluate CMs with the default level of "meets expectations" and trusted their intuition to guide them to shift that score upwards or downwards based on their interactions with the CM. Attendance just didn't leap out as remarkable either way, at least not without checking records. Worst of all for Rudy, he had no idea he was supposed to be awarded a license plate for his attendance. It was only discovered two years later, when our department manager Tanya cleaned out her desk to move to a different part of the park.

Park Anniversary Buttons

One of the easiest ways to engender a feeling of community among the Cast is to jointly celebrate. We saw this every year on the anniversary of Disneyland's opening, July 17. Cast Members were issued buttons for this day, proclaiming "We're

40 years old today!" (or whatever anniversary it was). In my early years, this wasn't a button, but a ribbon. As noted earlier, the very day of my Orientation—my first paid day of work—was July 17, 1987, so right from the start my Disney career was steeped in tradition and the company history. And I remain oddly proud of my ribbon declaring that "We're 32 today!"

Disneyland Line

The weekly newsletter for Disneyland CMs went a long way toward creating that feeling of family by doing constant stories on the people and locations around the park. One week it would be the Emporium's turn, next week would be Space Mountain. Whenever a ride or location was new, it got the premium treatment. It was a point of pride to have a photo of yourself in the Disneyland Line. Usually this would take the form of a quick posed photo right in the workplace, in costume.

My moment in the spotlight came about by accident. I was lounging around outside the CM check-in point, Harbor House, when someone approached me and asked if I'd like to be on the cover of the Disneyland Line. She wanted to stage a shot of people taking alternative transportation to work, so she wanted a photo of cars full of carpoolers and people riding a bicycle in the background. I was lent a bicycle to become one of the cyclists in the photo.

Tours of the Disney Studio and WDI

One of the greatest benefits of working for Disneyland was that I could take part in organized tours of the Walt Disney Studios or Walt Disney Imagineering. These seemed to take place about once a year—in the spring, if I recall correctly—and cost a nominal amount of money for the bus ride. Once there, we'd be treated to a guided tour of the facilities. This was my first introduction to the Walt Disney Archives in Burbank. Its well-known archivist, David Smith, gave the Archives life. Back in the 1960s, he approached Disney about organizing their materials. Incredibly, before this there was little organization to their libraries and collections, though obviously some stuff had been saved. By 1970, the Archives had been formed, with Dave as its head.

Dave showed us a valuable 1955 Opening Day ticket to Disneyland, and mentioned that he displayed it to all Disneyland groups. I don't recall most of the other items he showed us, but I do remember the collection being incredibly diverse: a Mickey Mouse tin from the 1930s, a Disneyland wall pennant from the '70s, a book on Disney movies. Dave stressed that they don't try to save absolutely everything at the archives, because they would quickly get overwhelmed. Instead, they try to create a representative collection of materials from given years, events, movies, and parks. Aspiring job hunters take note: Dave only hires someone with a master of library and information science (MLIS) degree, and as a rule he doesn't hire anyone who is a Disney fan— apparently there is too much temptation to steal something valuable.

Walt Disney Imagineering (WDI) is in a different city than the Studios, which has less to do with running out of space than it did with Disneyland's construction. When Walt pulled more and more of his creative Studio workers to the theme park project, the unions complained, and Walt decided it would be simpler to move the project off-site and permanently reassign some of his most talented folks. So WDI moved out to Glendale, near Interstate 5 and Griffith Park (the same Griffith Park where a carousel once inspired Walt to build Disneyland in the first place). My memory of WDI rests mainly on the scale models we saw strewn about on our visit. The Disneyland Space Mountain model (seen several years later at the Disney Gallery) was at that time in the lobby of WDI, and I was entranced. We were guided through buildings dedicated to show production, and I was flabbergasted that the entire place was peppered with props, models, signs, and sculpted miniature figures called maquettes.

Most of the actual offices and working spaces were unremarkable, aside from the amazing props and models lying about. A cubicle is a cubicle, after all. But WDI also boasts rooms (and sometimes entire buildings) full of scale models, sometimes of entire parks. Back then, EPCOT was only six years old, and the Disney/MGM Studios was a year away from completion, so we were enchanted at looking at the large model for the upcoming park. Such huge projects require an enormous amount of working space.

One other area we looked at was MAPO, which in those days was housed on-site with WDI (it moved at one point later to the nearby city of Tujunga, but eventually moved back). MAPO ostensibly stood for something to do with "manufacture" and "production," but the letters really came about because of MAry POppins, since the success of that movie created enough funds to build this production shop. This was where the one-of-a-kind designs for rides, vehicles, props, and Audio-Animatronics came to manufactured life. Most of WDI is given over to concepts and design, but in this corner, things were actually being built.

I would later visit both the Studios and WDI multiple times, but these first visits really cemented the magic for me. The company had little to lose by offering these to us rank-and-file folks, and a great deal to gain. We became more firmly ensconced in the corporate culture and vision after our visit, and it went a great deal toward meeting our own dreams, too. It was a real win-win for everyone.

Cast Showings of Movies

In the early 90s, there was a tendency to show all of the summer Disney movies, including those from the new Touchstone label, to the Disneyland Cast for free. Especially back then, that was a lot of movies per year. When the summer movie festival rolled around each year, the list of available movies showed up in the Disneyland Line, and one could obtain free tickets at Company D. I recall movies being shown first at the Lincoln theater on Main Street—a highly strange experience, since an attraction usually operated there—and later at Videopolis (later renamed Fantasyland Theatre). It didn't cost Disney much to put this on for Cast Members, but the gesture was really appreciated. We hard-working front line employees got to save a bit of money, while management took comfort in knowing the Cast was still highly in touch with the Disney product, a desirable outcome since these were the folks in daily contact with the Guests.

Flashback

The drive for community led to the creation in the late 90s of a CM-produced talent show called Flashback. Teams would form, usually within departments, to perform a skit or musical number on stage. Conceived as a way to let CMs speak their common language to each other in a fun way, the event also generated money for charity by selling tickets.

Arthur Holmson

Oddly, one of the best indicators that Disneyland was a family came from the outside. An elderly Guest named Arthur Holmson visited Disneyland every day, or at least it seemed so, and he knew a great many CMs by name, and others by appearance (I fell into the latter category). If he saw me in costume, he'd come over to chat for a few minutes. If he saw me out of costume but inside the park, he'd ask if I was "off" today. Leaving aside the oddness of the question—what else would I be doing in the park—it was always endearing, first because the question was so traditional as to be almost a ritual, and second because Arthur recognized my face.

Arthur, it turns out, was an institution at Disneyland. He'd been visiting for years, doing this same daily visit, moving slowly around the park with his cane and a large bag. I'd always heard that his intent was to collect items left by accident and return them to Lost and Found, just to be a nice guy. I'd also heard that Arthur was one of only two or three people that the folks at the Main Gate let in for free, no pass needed (one rumor I never believed was that he had known Walt personally). I never learned who the other folks were that supposedly got into the park for free. If there were others, Arthur would have loomed large over them anyway. He knew people in every ride, in every shop, and in every restaurant.

During the second year of Minnie's Moonlit Madness, the event was kicked off in Town Square, with organizers and a costumed Minnie Mouse up on the train station. Giving us all the signal to "go" was a surprise guest: Arthur himself. I never appreciated Arthur as a living legend until that moment, when I saw the crowd of CMs positively roar with approval that Arthur was here, supporting our CM-only event. Was there any further proof needed that Disneyland was a family? Walt was assuredly the patriarch of the clan when he was alive, and his void was still keenly felt by the time I arrived.

But Arthur had a role to play, too, something akin to the sentimental heart. When he died in 1992, things were never really the same again.

The Happiest Backstage on Earth

There are Backstage areas behind almost every location at Disneyland. To gain a clear view of the layout, we will simply take a complete round-trip tour of the back areas of the park, starting with Harbor House, where the CMs clocked in and clocked out of work. I'm providing a tour of the Disneyland Backstage as it existed in 1996.

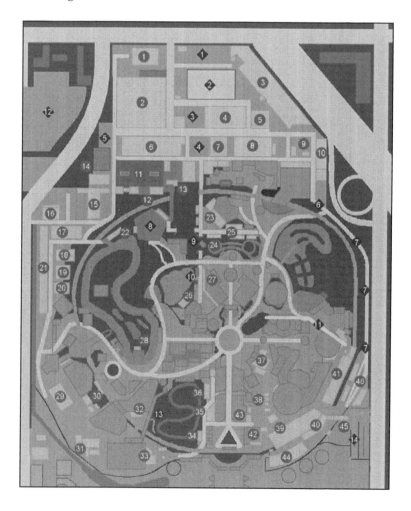

Map Key

Circles (buildings)
1. Property Control
2. Shipping and Receiving
3. Team Disney Anaheim (TDA)
4. Building 500 (maintenance bays)
5. Eat Ticket
6. Parade Building
7. Magic Music Days rehearsal hall
8. N-19 Entertainment Production Building
9. Landscaping
10. Roundhouse
11. Circle D Corral
12. Fireworks Shed
13. Owen Pope house
14. Landscaping
15. Resort Parking and Transportation (gas station)
16. N-7 Building: Maintenance costuming and lockers
17. Paint Shop
18. Staff Shop
19. Cycle Shop
20. Sign Shop
21. Mill
22. Fantasmic! Dry Dock
23. Fantasyland Theater Backstage
24. Additional Dressing Room
25. Casey Jr. and Storybook storage
26. Big Thunder maintenance bay
27. Village Haus backstage and food window
28. Fantasmic! descending stage
29. Outdoor Vending (ODV) headquarters
30. West Chiller Plant
31. Disneyland Design Studios

Map Key (continued)

32. New Orleans Square underground complex
33. Indiana Jones Adventure vehicle repair bay
34. Main Street Vehicle storage
35. Document Control
36. Jungle Cruise boat storage
37. Inn Between
38. Disneyland Center
39. Admin building, Costuming, Security
40. Disney University, Central Scheduling
41. Men's and Women's Upstairs Lockers, Head Room, Cast Cutters, Cash Control
42. Fire Station
43. Break room
44. H-5: new Costuming building (opened 2000)
45. Harbor House
46. East Chiller Plant, Company D, Credit Union

Diamonds (non buildings)
1. TDA visitor parking
2. TDA parking structure
3. Ball Gate
4. Prop Graveyard
5. Winston Gate
6. Parade crossing at the train tracks
7. Schumacher Road
8. Festival Theater
9. Tunnel to Fantasyland
10. Fantasyland Dumpster
11. Tomorrowland Tunnel
12. Ball Cast Member Lot (BCML)
13. Jungle Cruise Backstage Access
14. Hotel Bus Parking

Harbor House was the beginning and end of a Cast Member's day. This elongated shack was designed to hold two things: the complete set of paper timecards of the entire hourly Cast, and about eight time clocks, into any one of which a timecard was inserted until a date/time stamp was imprinted on the card. Payment was made in increments of 0.1 hours, so for an hour to be divided into ten parts, each segment had to last six minutes. CMs would clock in long before the start of their shifts, but at the end of their shifts, they did not clock out early or else they would lose pay. If they arrived before the designated end of their shifts, courtesy of the "walking time" that let them leave their work locations early, they congregated around the time clocks, waiting for the mechanical arms to tick forward. Every few minutes, a minor crowd would build up until the next six-minute increment was reached, setting off a brief rush to punch timecards and go home.

In the late 80s, the paper timecards were ditched, and new CM ID cards were issued that contained a barcode (still later, a yet new card system was issued that used a magnetic strip), and this enabled us to "clock in" by just swiping a card into several readers scattered about Harbor House.

Since everyone passed through this building, it was used as the distribution point for the weekly newsletter Disneyland Line, as well as the Cast Member Reference Guide, a detailing of the day's shows, character appearances, and other occurrences that were not published in the Guest version of the Disneyland Today brochure.

As one exited Harbor House on the other end, one saw a walkway that dipped down under the Disneyland Railroad. This was a covered trestle that marked the zone between the Grand Canyon and Primeval World dioramas. On our right side of the sidewalk was a street that made a similar dip. At the end of the dip was a T-intersection; the building directly in front of us was partly integrated with the back side of Space Mountain. At many times of year, the blank wall of the T-intersection was taken over by a chart showing how much cash the current charity fundraising effort had yielded, or how many Guest compliments had been achieved, or some similar measure.

Heading left at the T-intersection, we saw the old Administration building stretching out to our left; we had been walking past another face of this building as we went under the dip. Straight ahead was a large open area; we'd entered the zone between Main Street and Tomorrowland. Accordingly, Space Mountain was to our right, and my first few times back here I marveled at this new view of the familiar mountain. The lower half of the circular building was largely unthemed: just a giant circle of blue metal plates joined together in up/down ridges like corrugated cardboard. The roof was completely themed and painted white, presumably because it was visible from outside the park, and the roof hung over the blue cylinder walls like a giant mushroom, or perhaps a cupcake.

This zone behind Main Street was always depicted in wall maps as a wooded area, but it was more or less a parking lot. A few lucky people parked their personal cars back here, though most of the bigwigs parked on the other side of the Administration building. A portion of this area was given over to parking for parade floats; the permanent storage for floats was all the way in the back of the park behind Mickey's Toontown and the floats either wound their way Backstage via a perimeter road after a performance, or they remained behind Main Street awaiting the second performance, when they would reverse direction and head back to "it's a small world."

In the middle of this parking lot was a cluster of portable buildings like one might see on the grounds of a public school. This was the Disneyland Center. In my early years it was the nerve center for Cast Activities, ticket distribution to CMs, and the general hangout. In those days before Company D, it was the central location for hourly CMs to buy or reserve anything.

Because of the Disneyland Center's cluster of buildings, the parking lot and its road traced a loop around the central cluster. Following this road to the right, after passing Space

Mountain, we came across a few entrances to the On Stage areas: one near the Space Mountain exit, and just a few feet away, one near the Star Tours entrance. We weren't supposed to do this when out of costume and just visiting the park as a Guest, but there have been times people used the Backstage connection to simply jump from one end of Tomorrowland to the other in a few seconds.

Continuing around the parking lot, we came next to a large eatery. This was the Inn Between, a CM-only restaurant attached to the backside of the Plaza Inn (in fact, they shared a large central kitchen). Its name combined several ideas: it was located "in between" Tomorrowland and Main Street, it referenced a particular job in the animation process of creating action "in between" major character movements (such people were called In-Betweeners), and its joint location with the Plaza Inn made the spelling of "Inn Between" a natural fit. For most of my years, it was a standard cafeteria with a tray slide and people behind the counter who made items fresh on the grill, or dished up today's entrée, or created sandwiches by hand. In the mid-90s, it changed to an experimental new style that wasn't yet in the On Stage restaurants. Called scramble-style, the idea was numerous self-serve "stations" (a couple stations still required a worker behind the counter) divided up into islands. Patrons visited each one they needed to, and then headed to a central bank of cashiers. This style of service would later be seen On Stage at Redd Rockett's Pizza Port, Rancho del Zocalo, and the Plaza Inn, among others. Until the New Orleans Square expansion, this was the only Cast restaurant on property (Walt himself was known to eat here, for instance), so it sold a wide variety of food. The menu item that sticks out most in my memory was self-serve Dole whips, for which we were charged by the ounce. But it was much cheaper than the On Stage food, as was the case for the entire menu. In the early 2000s, the Cast restaurants were converted to a concept called Star Dinerz to bring uniformity to the various eateries, and prices mostly jumped upward. Later still they were outsourced to an external vendor named Sodexho.

Across from the Inn Between was another wooden building, labeled with a simple character sign as Central First Aid (CFA). This was a CM-only side to CFA; the Guest version of first aid was merely the opposite side of the same building, with the two halves never seeing each other. CFA was good for dispensing free aspirin and the like, and it also functioned as the place we turned in our doctor's notes when we missed more than three days of work in a row. There was always a nurse on duty here, and during the daytime hours there was a physician too. When I made the jump from seasonal work to permanent weekend work, I had to undergo a physical examination, and it took place here in CFA.

Don't Forget!

Appointment Date/Time:

_____

Health Services Phone Number:
(714) 781-4444
FAX (714) 781-4444

©Disney

D-1841 R-3

The doctor and nurses also tended to scrapes and bruises. When I scratched myself badly on a metal cash box, naturally I had to report this to CFA, and their response was to administer a tetanus shot to me right there. CFA makes the call on when to involve the paramedics or the local hospital, but they can handle a surprising amount of stuff right there. I even recall a couple of cots in the back where one could simply recuperate from injury or temporary nausea before returning to work.

Continuing the loop, we came to a covered outdoor break area containing simple tables and benches, an ATM, vending machines, and an arcade-style video game (I think it was some kind of violent two-person martial arts game) set to "free play." This area tended to be heavily used by the Character department, since just around the corner was the entrance On Stage to Town Square, where so many costumed characters met with Guests. When they escaped Backstage (at least fifteen minutes out of every hour), they took off their heads and hung out in this break area.

Just on the other side of the Town Square road—this was also the location of the double gates which swung open to let parade floats on and offstage—was the backside of the Opera House, where the Lincoln presentation was shown. Attached to the back end of this was the real fire department at Disneyland; the On Stage one in Town Square was just for show. The real fire department contained Disneyland's own fire fighting force, not run by the Anaheim Fire Department. There were fire marshals and inspectors, and a couple of modern fire trucks that I never once saw in use.

The loop around the parking lot finished its circle with the large Administration building, now on our right. This building was located "inside the berm" separating Disneyland from the outside world on purpose, so the park managers would be encouraged to go On Stage daily to witness what works (and what doesn't work) from the Guest perspective. Until the late 90s, this was the only administration building at Disneyland, but the three floors of offices held more than vice-presidents, accountants, and marketing teams. The side facing the parking lot held Casting and all the interview rooms. Up one floor was the Disney University, there to train the CMs once they were hired. The building also housed the Primeval World diorama right in the middle of the structure. That formed a natural separation to the two sides of the building. In the basement was a tunnel going under the diorama, so one could transition from the Disney University over to the parking lot by the Disneyland Center. This tunnel contained something very exciting for a geek like me: there was a timeline display of Disneyland's history through the decades, with photos and actual artifacts in the display cases on both sides of the tunnel. This was a fascinating way to go to work (some people used this tunnel from Harbor House; others were down here because of a locker room in the basement) since the whole thing was a bit of a museum, and it also reinforced the importance of history in the company's culture. It was finally removed in 2007.

Elsewhere on the Backstage side of the administration building were offices geared toward the operation of the park. On one far end of the second floor was Key Control, a place that held records, and in many cases duplicates, of all the keys used throughout the park. That was an intimidating room to enter, but I never went there except to have a duplicate made.

Directly below Key Control, and opposite the Fire Department, was Security. This suite of offices occupied the corner of the building and included not only the central office for the foot soldiers in the park, but also Central Communications, the radio hub of Disneyland operations. Communications answered the calls of 911 from in-park phones, they paged people over the radio network, and they issued "all calls" to all the radios in the park. If we needed radios for our events in New Orleans Square Restaurants, I'd go there to check them out temporarily. We followed police-style radio codes when talking on the open airwaves. The most important codes heard were:

101 – Attraction broken down

104 – Attraction resuming normal operations

10-21 – "please call the following phone extension." Example: "Jenny, please 10-21 Kevin at 5574."

10-87 – "meet me at the following location." Example: "Carrie, please 10-87 Kevin at the Veranda."

Code 1 – CFA was being dispatched somewhere in the park, but for a routine call. Security tended to accompany nurses, who invariably came with a wheelchair, whether it was wanted or not.

Code 2 – CFA run with some urgency; paramedics are possibly involved and may or may not come On Stage.

Code 3 – CFA run in an immediate life-threatening emergency. Code 3s are uncommon and translate to "get there *right now* to try to save a life (or do crowd control because there is a huge mess)."

Code 90 – The temperature had broken 90 degrees and CM restrictions eased (i.e., in our location, that meant bowties could be removed and the top shirt button unbuttoned).

Code 100 – The temperature had broken 100 degrees and still more procedures kicked in. At our restaurant, themed vests were removed and water could be consumed On Stage (normally drinking anything On Stage, even water, was verboten in those days).

Communications was also the place where the "keys to the kingdom" were stored overnight. There was a single set of keys—perhaps only eight in all—that were skeleton keys for every lock at Disneyland. They were held by whomever was in temporary charge of the park, called Ops1 (later renamed Duty Manager 1, or DM1, and later still Theme Park 1). The idea behind having a duty manager was that someone had to exercise the minute-by-minute decision-making that had park-wide effects. For instance, on slow days a certain restaurant might wish to close, but only the duty manager would know that all other nearby restaurants had already closed, and something would need to stay open. I had the privilege of once returning the DM1 keys to Security. It took a great deal of effort to resist the temptation to explore on my way to Security from the West Side. After all, the park was closed and deserted!

Disney fans often inquire about the concept of the Disneyland jail. There is no such place, at least not in the form commonly imagined. The suite of offices at Security includes several holding cells that are really just windowless rooms with white walls and no decorations or theming, and a table and chairs to conduct interviews. If needed, people could be kept inside these rooms while awaiting the arrival of the Anaheim Police Department (APD), who needed to be present before any real arrest could take place. In the post-9/11 world, APD became a constant presence at Disneyland, but in the old days, APD was summoned only when needed.

Security officers carried no weapons; only radios and their wiles. When there was a problem, they reacted by showing up in force. People sometimes resisted detention, others denied stealing and feared the arrival of APD, and still others were just belligerent. I happened to be walking by one day when a violent altercation broke out just in front of Security. A thirty-something man, held on both his upper arms by security officers, protested loudly about brutality while his wife and young daughter cowered off to the side. He broke free with one arm and smashed his fist against one officer's face, at which point the other officer and he began trading punches. The fracas brought an immediate reaction from inside Security as officers spilled out and overpowered the man. He was spread-eagled on the ground, with even his head held down, in a few moments, while his wife and child wailed. I walked on, knowing APD would arrive in a few minutes, and this man would spend the rest of his vacation behind very real bars. I never did find out what he was initially accused of, but his transgression while Backstage was enough to ensure he wouldn't just leave after making a statement.

The other half of the bottom floor in the Administration building was taken up by Men's Costuming. There were ten windows here, with different departments and divisions assigned to their own windows. Those of us in Foods, for instance, went to windows 1 through 4. In my early years, this was alphabetical; since my last name began with Y, I used window 4. I went to a certain window based on need: if I needed a *costume exchange* (just clean versions of the same costume pieces I was bringing back), I could use window 1, where the line went very fast. If I needed a *costume change* (I turned in my old costume, the paperwork was verified and then ripped up, and a new style of costume was issued with new paperwork), then I used window 3 or 4. This line moved more slowly because the process was so involved. Window 2 was also for costume exchanges, but only for Attractions and other departments, not Foods.

A costume exchange was a one-for-one process. If I wanted a new shirt and new pants, I had to bring the old shirt and the old pants with me. Often, some external costume pieces were only exchanged infrequently, like a bowtie or jacket, or even a vest, since they didn't get quite as dirty. Here's a similar workaround that now strikes me as unhygienic, but was common at the time: many folks needed to wear black socks with their costume, and since socks and shoes were the only parts of the costume not supplied by the company, that meant we needed our own supply of black socks. To avoid having to wash a pair every day, some folks would wear white socks and pull black socks on over the white ones, thinking that the black socks could then be used a second day before they needed cleaning.

CMs had lockers in this Backstage area, and the costumes would live in these lockers whenever the CM was not at work. I could choose to exchange my costume at the end of my shift, and then leave the fresh costume on hangers in my locker for my next shift, since it was always nice to plan ahead in case I might be late. I sometimes did this when I had a 7:30 a.m. shift the next morning, since mornings were busier at Costuming, and I was always slow to wake up anyway and might be running late. The company tried to persuade most workers to make this exchange at the end of a shift, which is why fifteen minutes of "walking time" was provided at the end of a working shift (in later years, this would become twenty minutes). If I was scheduled to be off work at 17:00 hours, I actually left my location at 16:45 hours. There was no walking time at the start of a shift; only at the end, and the ostensible purpose was to pay CMs for the time they took to exchange a costume, because the company didn't want employees wearing soiled costumes On Stage the next day. And even an exchange could take the full fifteen minutes, because I first had to go to my locker, change into my street clothes, take the soiled items I wanted exchanged down to costuming, wait in line, hand over the clothes to request new ones, and then return those to my locker.

The actual process of exchange consisted of handing over the shirt and pants to an attendant behind the window and verbally requesting the desired sizes—in my case, 15 ½ for the shirt and 30-32 for the pants in those days. I was always amazed at the speed of some of these Costuming workers who took my old clothes, whipped them into segregated duffel bags, and darted off to get me fresh versions. They were also pretty adept at making sure I got the exact right versions: some shirts looked alike but weren't, and many sets of pants had similarities but weren't really identical. Those similar-but-different costume pieces could come in handy if my normal sizes were "sold out" from their supply, an occurrence that unfortunately happened all too often. If they didn't have my size, I could try to request "near" sizes, which would result in too-tight or too-loose articles of clothing. If that didn't work, I could use the look-alike costume pieces. In the worst-case scenario, I could also take back my slightly dirty costume pieces and simply wear them again the next day.

The process of a "full costume change" was necessary when I needed to work in a different location that had a different costume. To make a full change, I had to return all the pieces issued to me and reconcile my account. In theory, I was supposed to be charged if an item was missing, but in practice, the workers often didn't notice, and even if they did, merely claiming that no such item was ever issued to me usually didn't meet with much of a challenge. After my record was cleared, a new costume could be issued to me. Here is where one relied upon the training and memory of the attendant. If the Costuming CM knew his stuff, he'd hear the name of the costume I requested and instantly assemble the right pieces. But there were dozens of costumes and permutations, even in Foods alone, so it wasn't surprising if new hires didn't quite know what to put in the costume. They sometimes consulted photos hung on the walls, or they asked me (or their own co-workers) for help, and sometimes they just guessed—meaning the hapless CM had to check what was delivered, to make sure the person wasn't guessing incorrectly.

Full costume changes were relatively common in my restaurant. There was the default costume, but also a "chef whites" version for folks working in the visible kitchen or in the downstairs prep area, and since we were all trained in these multiple locations, we often had to do costume changes from shift to shift. This was annoying mostly because service at the full-change windows was invariably slower. That had to do with the way Costuming was staffed. Though there were ten windows, there were usually only one or two workers behind the windows, and they shuttled back and forth to the windows wherever needed. Often, that was just fine; most windows were usually empty. When I arrived at a window with a line, I knew I'd be served when I got to the front. But if the window was empty when I arrived, the attendants needed to know someone was there, so I touched a button on the wall that rang a bell and put me into an electronic queue. This was almost never necessary at the exchange windows, which had a constant, though small, line, and thus essentially a full-time attendant. But it was always necessary at the full-change windows. I once watched one CM ring the bell repeatedly, but he became frustrated that it only made a chime the first time, and was silent once in the electronic queue, no matter how often he rang the outside button. He reached around the window to the button on the attendant's side that acknowledged the window was now staffed and pressed it, and he realized that he could now make a noise by ringing the outside button again. So he pushed both buttons alternately to maintain an incessant buzz, thinking this would surely get attention. Several minutes later, a breezily grinning Costuming CM arrived and told him such action was merely resetting the window's position in the electronic queue over and over, and the window would *always* be the last one to be served—no wonder it took so long on that day!

The other windows were dedicated to different departments and divisions, and I never needed to visit them, except for window 10. This last window was used to issue nametags. When I was first hired, my nametag was given to me at Orientation, but if I needed to replace it, this was the window I went to. One first had to pay $5 and then could place an order for a nametag with the right name on it (no nicknames were allowed), and it would be ready in a few days. In the meantime, they offered a loaner nametag with any old name on it. We could just hunt through the bin until we found an identity that would be nice to assume for a few days. This was also the procedure if I thought my nametag had slipped off and it might have been picked up by a CM and returned to this central location; that way I wouldn't have to buy a new one. Window 10 was also the place I'd bring my paperwork for a new "award" nametag, such as the free one we received when we reached the one-year or five-year milestones.

With the construction of Disney's California Adventure, the addition of so many new CMs called for a new costuming system entirely, since the old one wouldn't be able to take on additional capacity. A new Costuming building was erected in September, 2000 outside Harbor House to sit in the space between the theme parks. In this new massive facility, there would be a self-service warehouse of costume pieces, and registers to check out the clothes. Barcodes made the process quick: I scanned in my old clothes (there was no more "exchange") and then scanned out the new ones after I hunted them down. Motorized conveyor belts made it simple to cycle through costume pieces of various types and sizes, and added to the futuristic feel of the endeavor. Upstairs, "day lockers" enabled CMs to change into work clothes and to have a place to store street clothes. But under the new system, very few people used the day lockers. Part of the change was the introduction of FastTrack, a new program of checking out costumes. Instead of being allowed only one complete costume set at a time, now CMs would be allowed several—up to four sets at the beginning. This way, they could dress at home and come to work already in costume. When the clothes were dirty, they could return them to be laundered, often several sets at a time. This may have led to more theft of costume pieces. In the old days, we were not allowed past Harbor House with any costume piece. FastTrack had been tested with the New Tomorrowland of 1998 and implemented for a wider audience in 2000.

Returning mentally to 1996 and continuing the tour of Backstage, finally reaching the end of the parking lot loop behind Space Mountain, we would see the extreme end of the Administration building. This end of the building was given over to Women's Costuming, and it was a much smaller area than the men's. It had fewer windows, only six in all. Thus it was an ironclad certainty that women always had to stand in longer lines than men. Whether that was a reflection of the sexism in society in the 50s, when the building was constructed, or some other operational happenstance (perhaps originally the Cast consisted of more men than women?), I never found out.

The area just in front of Women's Costuming was used to store large duffel bags stuffed full of soiled costumes, which would be picked up en masse by the outside vendor who laundered all of the costumes. In the meantime, these bags provided a popular place to lounge about while waiting for friends to change back into their street clothes at the end of the day. The bags were comfortable! While the costumes inside may be considered soiled, they weren't particularly smelly. After all, they were changed every day, at least in theory, so they had little opportunity to get ripe.

Crossing the street that led under the railroad tracks and back out to Harbor House, one came across another building similar in size to the administration building. The back half of this building housed the Grand Canyon Diorama. The front end was once home to an ancillary locker room, though its function changed over time. Next up along the building was a shoe shine chair, much like one in an airport. Though sometimes unstaffed, there was often the same young African-American boy here, waiting for a chance to shine shoes for a couple of bucks. Immediately after the shoe shine was Cast Cutters, a barber shop just for CMs. I used a barber close to my house who was slightly cheaper, but I now regret not having my hair done at least once by the Disneyland guys. Their advertising always promised that no one would know "the Disney Look" quite like they would, and I'm sure that's true.

Next came the Entertainment Head Room, which presumably was where the costumed characters picked up their heads—it was never clear to me if the rest of their costumes were in here too, and one didn't venture into this space without a reason to be there.

On both sides of the Head Room were staircases; one going up to the Women's Upstairs Lockers and one going up to the larger Men's Upstairs Lockers. In addition to these locker zones, there was another Women's Locker Room across the way in the large Space Mountain building (this part of it was just shaped like a rectangular building, not like Space Mountain), and there was a Men's Downstairs Lockers in the administration building, accessed via the previously-described timeline tunnel.

The lockers were arranged much like high school athletic lockers: benches in the middle and communal showers off to one corner for the men, and individual showers in the women's locker rooms. Very few people used these showers, though one older gentleman from Security used them daily. He sticks out in my memory because he would dress in his costume after the shower without putting on any underwear, and that's an image one doesn't forget easily. Since these costume pieces were worn by everyone sooner or later, I sometimes wondered if the other Security CMs knew their pants may have been worn previously by someone without underwear.

Every year there was a "locker clear out" which was announced some weeks ahead of time. The idea was that miscellaneous costume pieces, including those that didn't actually belong to the CMs in question, would accumulate in the locker over time, and a forced check that the locker was completely empty was the only way to ensure that things didn't get out of hand. On such days, we had to return our costumes completely so that we had nothing checked out to us. We knew to take all our personal items out of the lockers, too, or else they would be confiscated and discarded. On the night of a locker clear-out, there would be chaos in the aisles. Giant piles of jackets, shirts, and other items that had been illegally stored sprouted up on the benches. I'm sure Security had to be extra vigilant as people left Harbor House, to make sure they weren't wearing those ill-gotten costumes. Some sneaky folks managed the feat by wearing their street clothes over the costume pieces. After all, there was no strip search as one left work for the day.

At the far end of the lockers building was Cash Management, though for most of my years it was known as Cash Control. This was, for all intents and purposes, the real bank at Disneyland. Cash Control was the place cashiers would start their day and check out a starting cash fund. At the end of the day, they'd return all their accumulated cash, checks, and credit card drafts here, too. Originally, this was pretty low-security; the counter was essentially open to the visiting CMs, with only a counter-to-ceiling grating providing safety. It always occurred to me that when the armored Brinks truck came, which seemed like a daily event, giant bags of money were reasonably within grasp of a dedicated thief. Apparently the company noticed the same thing, for when the facility was renamed Cash Management, it got a security upgrade. The counter area became protected by thick bulletproof glass. I never saw the coin room and the vault, but I assume they received hefty security upgrades as well.

Just outside the locker building was a super-sized shed that functioned as the home base for Outdoor Vending (ODV). In those days, ODV had several popcorn stands that didn't move, a few mobile carts for ice cream, and vendors who would hold balloons by hand. In the morning hours, one heard a lot of balloons popping as they were over-inflated in this ODV shed. In later years, ODV would grow as a department. Many more mobile carts would be added, and ODV would move to a new location behind Splash Mountain.

This was effectively the dead-end of the Backstage area in this half of the park, next to the then-empty Carousel Theater (which would later house Innoventions). One small non-descript door here at the base of the carousel provided the continuation of our tour. It led to an underground tunnel which ran out to Tomorrowland Terrace (it was unrelated to a parallel tunnel that would later be built to house the Rocket Rods queue). It was a fairly boring tunnel, with bare concrete walls, somewhat narrow, and a whole mess of tubes and pipes running overhead, at least one of them labeled as containing water from the submarine lagoon.

From Tomorrowland Terrace, however, there were no connecting tunnels out to the rest of Disneyland. It's the Magic Kingdom in Florida, not Disneyland, which has the Utilidors, a system of interconnected underground passageways. Here at Disneyland, we had to surface On Stage in Tomorrowland. To continue our tour, we'd have to make our way over to Fantasyland, where the zone behind the Village Haus was another Backstage island, bordered on other sides by Big Thunder Mountain Railroad, Carnation Plaza Gardens, the Frontierland Shootin' Gallery, and Casa Mexicana. Back here was a minor open space that I associated with an annual SPAM-Fest put on by the chefs in each of the lands. Every chef would create dishes that included SPAM, and the rank-and-file CMs were invited to taste all the dishes and choose a winner.

In an open-air alley between the Village Haus and Big Thunder was a dumpster and break area, but what always caught my eye was a wooden tower hidden amid tall trees, reaching up a few stories toward the sky. This was the terminus of the tightrope from the Matterhorn, where Tinker Bell ended her slide during the fireworks shows. It's the stuff of CM legend to watch this occur, and a small crowd gathered at the base each night. The Tinker Bell performer had a handbrake, and she slowed herself down as best she could when she approached the end of the rope. Around that time, the spotlight on her went out, as the park didn't want the general population to see her as she landed. And with good reason, because the landing was somewhat violent. Despite her handbrake, she was still going fast when she came to the small platform at the top of the wooden tower. Four men, holding the corners of a specially-designed mattress, caught her in this giant makeshift catcher's mitt, and she would slam to a stop. She would later climb down the tower, don a large overcoat, slip back On Stage, and melt into the crowd on her way back home. In later years, the fireworks show would call for an entire array of wires able to send Tinker Bell in both directions. Since the performer could slow down completely and even change directions, the need for a platform disappeared, and the tower was transformed to an oversized artificial tree.

The Village Haus was home to some Backstage offices and corridors, and by following these, one came across a hidden food window. Off to the far side of the regular Guest-service counter windows was a CM-only service of the Village Haus food, and at rock-bottom prices. Since its menu was so limited, and the location was hidden anyway, there were seldom lines here.

The Village Haus also sported a very minor underground complex. Most of its kitchen was upstairs, but there were storerooms, break rooms, and offices downstairs. There's a persistent urban legend that this underground connects to Tomorrowland, but that's merely wishful thinking.

The last item of note in this Backstage complex, back up on ground level, was the home base for the entire Custodial department, including all the sweepers, bathroom attendants, and many of the bussers for the restaurants park-wide. Their office, attached to the Casa Mexicana building, was always bustling, as befits a department with so many Cast Members moving in so many different directions.

We could exit out into Frontierland through a swinging door that sat unmarked between the Shooting Gallery and Casa Mexicana (now Rancho del Zocalo). The next Backstage island was in Adventureland, though one border of this extremely narrow Backstage space consisted of the other row of buildings in Frontierland. We could enter near the Adventureland restrooms (at least until a 1994 rehab removed this entrance), or by a gate by Stagedoor Café, or by a gate next to Bengal BBQ. Most of this Backstage island was unremarkable. It was over-crowded with carts and cans and equipment, and one marveled that they could squeeze a dumpster in here. But upstairs, essentially over the River Belle Terrace, was a major nexus for the park. This was the Adventureland Area Office, which was really the major office for the whole of the west side of the park. The abbreviated land names were found on the office lettering: "Adv/Fr/NO/CC Area Office." The area manager for this section of the park had his office here—in my day, the area manager was Ray. This was also the distribution center for the paychecks for all of us who worked in Adv/Fr/NO/CC. Every

Wednesday, we'd be there in line to pick up our paychecks. Occasionally one would also have to come here to pick up tickets for special or free events, in the days before such operations were centralized at Company D or TEAM Centers.

Skipping On Stage again briefly to the last Backstage island, we came to New Orleans Square. This Backstage area was unique because it was apparently underground, not at the same level as the Guests. But that's not entirely correct. If one paid attention to the ground rising slowly as visitors On Stage neared New Orleans Square, one might not be surprised to discover that what looks like ground level is actually the second floor. The real ground level was now underground and formed a bustling complex of Foods operations, with a centralized kitchen and related operations, including a midsized Backstage cafeteria. Winding its way around this complex, in some ways twisted together, were the track and show rooms of Pirates of the Caribbean, though parts were also contained in a show building out behind the land and near the train tracks.

The remaining Backstage areas at Disneyland in 1996 ringed the perimeter of the park. I've already described the area behind Main Street East that runs up to Tomorrowland, and if we started at Main Street West and worked our way around the outside of the park, we could trace a giant horseshoe shape, ending up in that same zone already described behind Tomorrowland.

Some visitors to Disneyland may have seen the Backstage of Main Street West already. This zone was sometimes used as an additional corridor to let folks exit the park in the summer of 1996, when crushing crowds bid adieu to the Main Street Electrical Parade. The end of the street is actually the back side of the Jungle Cruise, and the Backstage dock and storage for the boats ran along one side of the street. This same side of the street was given over elsewhere to tents for the

Horsedrawn Streetcars. The other side of the street was dominated by the nondescript back sides of the Main Street buildings, since they were purely functional in form.

As one passed the turn back to Town Square (this was the exit taken by Guests allowed back here in 1996), the road ahead curved to the right and continued to frame the Jungle Cruise. The road also dipped precipitously—we needed to pass underneath the Disneyland Railroad, and the road rose back up again afterward. An unmarked and unthemed zone ensued: the Main Gate infrastructure and Guest lockers were located on one side, with jungle on the other side. The hippo pool, skipper gunshot, and chanting natives ("ah ah ah… oh oh ohhh, oh weiii") were quite audible back here. I've known CMs who waited for the crack of a capgun, then yelled "Ow!" as loudly as they could, hoping the Guests in the boats would hear them.

Prior to the mid-90s, it was a straight shot back here to the New Orleans turnoff—we had to go down another incline and go under the train again—or we could continue onward around the perimeter. But the introduction of the Indiana Jones Adventure in 1995 meant that the perimeter road pushed out far around the new building, which took over the former Eeyore parking lot. In those years, the old Disneyland parking lot was otherwise still there, so a "crow's nest" watch tower was constructed atop Indiana Jones, to look out for crime over the parking lot below. Even after Disneyland's expansion meant the removal of the parking lot, the crow's nest remained atop the building. For CMs walking to work and wishing to avoid walking all the way around the Indy building, a wooden bridge with lots of steps was constructed over the Indy queue, which reached all the way outside the berm.

Staying on the perimeter, one first passed the Indy building and the Pirates building on the right and then came upon the Haunted Mansion building, also on the right. The fence separating the parking lot from this Backstage area was a plain chain-link fence, and one opening called Holiday Gate, though usually locked, provided easy access to the Rivers of America for early morning canoe race teams. Holiday Gate was so named because, in the 1950s, this area of the parking lot had been home to a corporate picnic area called Holidayland. Holidayland used the same circus tent that had been in the park as the Mickey Mouse Club Circus.

A chiller plant nearby provided air-conditioning services to this half of the park, and "portable" trailers on the other side of the perimeter road were used as a forward base of operations by Walt Disney Imagineering (WDI), in a sub-division called the Disneyland Design Studio (DDS). The DDS trailers were adorned with signs for rides and shows they had built, such as one for "Imagination," the original name of Fantasmic! when it was under development.

The perimeter road then took a couple of turns around Splash Mountain and the DDS parking lot, though the parking lot was frequently filled with logs from the ride that were being reconditioned. Around the back side of Splash Mountain was a narrow road that cut deep into Critter Country, part of it as a tunnel. This led straight to the back area of Hungry Bear Restaurant and ended at a door On Stage, next to the downstairs bathrooms.

Back at the main perimeter road, we passed by several services and crafts. Here was the sign shop, which made signs (especially replacement signs and menus) for all locations in the park. The paint shop back here seemed expansive to me, with lots of space and workstations to paint just about anything. The nearby staff shop took its name from the studio designers who built Disneyland; in Hollywood studios, the staff shop makes moldings and the like. Out here was also a mill, a metal shop, and just about everything else one could think of.

Around a corner one came across a vehicle repair facility. Here they fixed mostly Backstage vehicles, and it bore the name Cycle Shop because ride vehicles were "cycled" through annual maintenance here. This was once the original roundhouse for the Disneyland Railroad, and rails in the road could still be seen. There was even evidence of that original roundhouse visible from On Stage; when making the final turn from the Rivers of America toward Fantasyland, visitors could turn around to the left and watch for a tunnel to nowhere. This was the original track for trains to join the main line.

Beyond this building was a small pedestrian and vehicle entry way known as Winston Gate, named after an original street that back in the 1950s bisected the property, called Winston Street. Because of Winston Street, the Pony Farm (now Circle D Corral) and maintenance areas were across the street from the park. At Winston Gate in my day, there was little traffic back here before the expansion of the Disneyland Resort. Later, the parking garage was added just outside Winston Gate, and the area was expanded.

Opposite the vehicle repair facility was a large central ramp to a circular platform, around which were several kinds of dumpsters for recycling. In the days before eBay and wholesale liquidators, this was the final resting grounds for old props and signs at Disneyland; I've seen many signs simply thrown away in these dumpsters.

Off to the side were sheds containing fireworks, if the many warnings on the sides of the sheds were to be believed. Scattered about in this vicinity of Backstage were fireworks launchers, including several atop raised platforms on metal towers that launched diagonally. The buildings around here had to be closed during fireworks; people were either forced to stay inside or warned to stay away from the area. One Entertainment building had a smoldering fireworks shell punch through its ceiling right to a second-floor office, so it wasn't entirely safe to be back here, even indoors. Minor fires were common, though quickly dealt with.

Just past the dumpster and the vehicle repair facility was a gas station for company vehicles such as pickup trucks that were used around the property. The gas was "free," though charged to the department later by virtue of an automated system.

Off to the right side of the road, and close to the dumpsters, was the large Backstage ranch where all the animals lived, known as the Circle D Corral. Mules used to live here when rides were available in Frontierland, and the Main Street horses continued to make this their home. Related vehicles also resided here, such as the Disneyland Stagecoach or seldom-used horse-drawn carriages.

An old dwelling in the Circle D Corral was said to be the last original house left on property, inhabited at one time by Owen Pope and his wife, Dolly. Pope was the man hired by Walt Disney to raise and train the mules and horses needed for Disneyland. In my days, this ramshackle wooden building still had peeling white paint and was used as offices by the Security forces who took care of the guard dogs. Nearby were the doghouses for the guard dogs, mostly German shepherds. Around the corner of the Pope house was a winding road that led up the berm, across the train tracks, and to the back side of the Festival Theater, home in 1996 to the Hunchback of Notre Dame Festival of Fools stage show.

Back on the perimeter road, one passed an enormously long building used to house the parade floats, and then one finally reached the corner of the property. From here only a right turn was possible, and we passed large warehouses that constituted the primary receiving center of Disneyland, where pallets full of wax cups, napkins, and most dry goods first came to the park.

On our left after the warehouse was a gap in the fence to the outside world, behind which Ball Road was visible. Accordingly, this was known as Ball Gate, and it was one of the primary ways vehicles came into the Backstage areas of Disneyland.

On the outside of Ball Gate lay the surface parking lot for short-term parking, as well as the parking garage for long-term parking for the Team Disney Anaheim (TDA) building. TDA was the "new" administration building opened in 1995 on the spot of the old Global Van Lines building. Metallic green on the public side of the building and canary yellow on the other, TDA was designed by Frank Gehry during Eisner's era of inventive architecture. Out front by the CM entrance was a PeopleMover car, left here as a reminder of the ride but also as a public bench. TDA was the new home of Casting and Orientation, in addition to the place where almost all the executives worked once the building was completed. Nearby was the Eat Ticket, a pun on E-Ticket. In keeping with this whimsy, from the ceiling were hung ride vehicles from old attractions such as the Motor Boat Cruise and the long-since-replaced Indian War Canoes.

Just inside Ball Gate and back along the outside perimeter road was a prop graveyard. Sitting here on open-air shelves, or just arranged on the blacktop itself, were props large and small from attractions that either closed down or had props replaced by newer versions. I can recall columns from Indiana Jones and many different pieces of the Submarine Voyage: mermaids, plastic fish, and that goofy serpent. After several years, they rotted and bleached in the sun, until finally Disneyland learned that each prop could bring in a lot of money on Internet auction sites such as eBay.

The next entire row of buildings was given over to warehouse-sized maintenance bays, where ride vehicles were overhauled and repaired, especially during an attraction's annual refurbishment. It was always somehow exciting to see Space Mountain sleds or Big Thunder Mountain Railroad trains sitting in an industrial setting, because the vehicles were familiar, but the context was so new.

The next building one row inward, away from the perimeter fence, was the Entertainment building. Here there was a separate wardrobe department, locker area, and several offices. Nearby, a mini-tractor and tram swung by every few minutes to shuttle costumed characters back and forth from here to the back side of Main Street East, so they could be close to the traditional spot for characters to appear in Town Square.

One final building inward toward the berm, adjacent to the Circle D Corral, was used by visiting high school bands to practice for the Magic Music Days program. The kids would be bussed to this point, they would practice indoors and await their big moment, and then walk from here into the park at Town Square, or they would enter near the point where Frontierland and Fantasyland met. The latter was accomplished by traveling on a road that went under the railroad track, first dipping down and then angling back up, and then opening onto a Backstage crossroads. To the left was the Backstage side of the Fantasyland Theatre, with a couple of access doors On Stage and a few dressing rooms underneath. A road just past the theater cut into the On Stage lands like a giant peninsula; it was once the back side of Fantasyland but later separated Fantasyland from the theater and Mickey's Toontown. At the end of that road was the Backstage parking for Casey Jr. trains, another sight that was strange the first few times I saw it.

Back at the crossroads, there were other choices. A tunnel cut through another earthen berm led to the kitchen side of Big Thunder Barbecue (later called Festival of Foods). This tunnel was interesting because the walls and ceiling were made out of a single giant corrugated aluminum tube.

While that corrugated aluminum tube was short, the final passage from the crossroads was another such tube, but this one traveled a much longer journey under the hill and trees, eventually leading out to the junction between Frontierland and Fantasyland, near the restrooms. The tunnel was big, designed to allow large trucks to pass through, because this was the method by which the Fantasyland Backstage was accessed. Large gates (also visible from On Stage) at the end of the tunnel were swung open, and similar gates on the other side of the On Stage walkway could be opened as well, and just like that, a clear path would be opened to the Village Haus restaurant for replenishing supplies or hauling out the dumpster.

Back on the other side of the railroad track, and near the Magic Music Days building, was still another set of warehouses. They had multiple functions and departments, but I associate this area most with a surplus facility for Disneyland. I once poked around here for some time trying to find a desk we could use as a new Lead desk at the French Market.

Across the way was the Landscaping department, where everything from potted plants to giant animal topiaries were grown, stored for trimming, or nursed back to health before they were returned to the park. Giant cranes used for landscaping work were also stored here.

One final road behind property control led back to the Magic Music Days building, but this one, closest to the On Stage area at Toontown, was different in that it was a one-way street (though that didn't quite make it completely unique; a few one-way streets dotted the area near the prop graveyard along the perimeter). As one traveled this road back to Magic Music Days, the Toontown backdrop loomed overhead, so that one essentially drove under the Toontown letters. It was jarring to see that the highly colored backdrop was elevated by unthemed, brown pylons located literally at the side of the road (it was quite narrow back there).

Back at Landscaping, one final building loomed large and dominated the area. Situated at the end of all these east-west Backstage roads was the roundhouse, home to the Disneyland Railroad on the first floor and the Monorail on the second floor. It was quite a sight to see all the locomotives and the cars stored in here in the early morning (or late at night). Seeing this kind of Backstage magic actually increased my appreciation of these vehicles when I saw them On Stage.

The monorails and train tracks crossed the winding perimeter road, and this area was also used to access the parade route. Just past this point, the parade route had to cross the train tracks, so riders of the Disneyland Railroad could catch a glimpse of this entire area and the roundhouse as they passed by the submarine service facility.

The main perimeter road then went around a sharp curve or two, and headed due south, to parallel Harbor Blvd. just on the other side of a very high fence. This section was called Schumacher Road and was named after a former Director of General Services for the park. Fred Schumacher had helped Disneyland secure enough extra land from the city of Anaheim to build a road between the berm and Harbor Boulevard. Schumacher Road wound around monorail pylons, so a drive along here involved a lot of weaving left and right. It, too, could be glimpsed by On Stage visitors who watched for it from the monorail.

Schumacher Road ended by first passing the east chiller plant and then coming upon several portables. One was used as a dedicated break area for kids who were bussed in from inner-city L.A., as part of a program to bring diversity to the Disneyland cast, and also to increase the pool of workers. Another was home to a credit union open only to Disneyland CMs, called Partners Federal Credit Union (in honor of the relationship between Walt and Mickey). This credit union preceded the Partners statue now at the hub, so the statue always reminded me of the credit union. The ATMs located throughout Backstage were Partners ATMs. In later years, Partners FCU moved off property.

Also gone now, but present in my day, was the original home of Company D, housed in another of the portables at the end of Schumacher Road. Company D opened during my tenure, and formed the first outlet for CMs to get park merchandise at a discounted rate. Prices were excessively low; I picked up a Grad Nite '88 T-shirt for twenty-five cents, still in its plastic wrapping. In later years, Company D became home to one of many so-called TEAM centers for tickets and special merchandise, and it eventually moved off the property.

The fence-bounded zone for the portables formed a central area that was sometimes used for a traveling truck selling appropriate work shoes. Essentially a store on wheels, it was touted as a great place to get Disneyland-approved footwear, though one wasn't required to use only those shoes.

Schumacher Road dead-ended at Harbor House, our staring point for the tour. The road took a sharp right turn to go under the train tracks, the previously described covered trestle that Guests may have recognized as the zone between the Grand Canyon diorama and the Primeval World. The road dipped down so sharply that it could be dangerous for drivers. I once saw a golf cart crashed at the bottom. The driver, a Disneyland security officer, lost control due to the increased speed and slammed into the pylon holding up the trestle. Sprawled on the ground, he was being treated where he lay. I always kept that poor guy in mind as I turned to go down this incline, and I slowed down. An accident, it seemed to me, could have been a real possibility otherwise.

Since we started at Harbor House, it seems fitting to end our tour here as well. After paper timecards were phased out, there were several transition years in which one swiped the ID card through a reader just to gain access to Harbor House, and then swiped a different time clock inside to clock in. When Disneyland expanded and added DCA, Harbor House was only used for pass-through, not timecard stamping, and was renamed Harbor Pointe. Cast Members swiped their ID cards through a reader in the quad to prove their current status, and that same swipe functioned as their electronic clock-in. All that was quite different from the experience in my early years, when one simply flashed the ID card, picture side out, to get access to Harbor House. Seems like pretty simplistic security in retrospect, but it was all that was needed to guard access to the happiest Backstage on Earth.

Innovation and Reinvention

Life as a Working Lead, at least at the Café, was much more than being a glorified "breaker." The Leads did control the break schedule, though in later years a computerized (and some say dehumanized) system called Cast Deployment System (CDS) was rolled out in some departments. CDS would optimize break schedules so that no CM would be robbed of breaks (an occurrence which could happen with incompetent Leads), and it took all the thinking out of the equation. CDS would issue a ticket, explaining who the CM should next replace. It was used not only for breaks, but also position rotation, to guarantee that no one got bored by working an entire shift in any one position.

As the person nominally in charge, the Lead made all the routine decisions. For instance, whenever something broke, it was the Lead who called out the correct facilities worker to fix things. There was a slight learning curve in knowing whom to call: Arcade (a department so named because they also fixed video games) repaired our computers, plumbers came for anything having to do with water or pipes, and machinists fixed moving parts like display cases. A/C was called not only for air conditioning, but also to fix ice machines (it was from them that I learned the complete history of the "falling rock" effect in the Indiana Jones Adventure—it was created by an ice machine, and the conveyor used to move the ice around had a reputation for breaking down often). Add to that list the metal shop, the staff shop, and landscaping, and you've got a confusing myriad of services to call. Having all of these support services spoils you. Whenever my refrigerator or dishwasher at home broke, the first thought always to flit across my consciousness was to pick up the phone and call for one of Disneyland's support units, which are, of course, free.

Non-emergency repairs were requested in a different fashion. Known as Shop Work Order Requests (incongruously given the acronym SWRs), in my later years these were phoned in to a central agency, and assigned a priority of 2-4 (a priority 1 was when the fix was to be immediate, and the support unit was called out right away). This is how burned-out light bulbs were reported, or a request was made to have some chipped paint re-touched. In my earlier years, these SWRs were hand-written on paper (in triplicate, of course), and then brought to a central location. On our side of the park, that location was the Lead's podium at the Jungle Cruise. Since I normally worked in a restaurant all day, it was a minor thrill to have actual business at an attraction, so it was always fun to run over to the Jungle Cruise and hand in a bundle of SWRs.

At a couple times during my years, at the Café we had our own Lead podium, but mostly I wanted the Lead to have a desk. This wasn't because I was lazy and wanted to spend all my time sitting, although some Leads did in fact stay sitting at the desk all the time, and that was a problem. I wanted it because the start-of-day and end-of-day calculations took a long time, as did the other paperwork, and standing that long would have been onerous. In the middle of my shift, I was always away from the desk, returning only to record the hourly sales figures on the operations sheet and crew roster for the day, abbreviated "Ops" sheet.

Wanting a Lead desk and obtaining one were two different things. One first had to acquire permission from the supervisors, and then obtain the actual desk from somewhere or other. Rather than buy new furniture, we scoured the available desks at property control, and managed to find one small enough to fit into the thin space next to the Café elevator. When I hired into the French Market some years later, this process would be repeated, and again it would be a challenge to find a small enough desk.

There were other special projects, things that didn't fall into the usual day-by-day routine of being a Lead, such as filling out performance appraisals for our CMs. For CRs and full-time CMs, a blank copy of a performance appraisal was circulated to all the Leads who worked with that person. We'd each fill out the appraisal individually, and the supervisor would then take all opinions into account as he or she wrote the final version to be given to the CM, usually around the CM's birthday.

For Casual-Temporary workers, the supervisors didn't write an appraisal at all. Each Lead would be given a stack of CT appraisals, and that Lead would be the only person who wrote an appraisal for those CMs. From the CT's point of view, it was the luck of the draw. If the Lead filling out the appraisal wasn't fair, there wasn't much the CT could do about it. Fortunately for the CT's, most of the time the notion of "grade inflation" was alive and well, as the Leads didn't want to have the face-to-face talk to explain worker deficiencies, and opted instead to provide at least the grade of 'meets expectations' for almost every category.

			4. EXCEEDS DISNEY STANDARDS	3. MEETS DISNEY STANDARDS	2. DOES NOT MEET DISNEY STANDARDS	1. DISREGARDS DISNEY STANDARDS
CASUAL/TEMPORARY DISNEYLAND PERFORMANCE APPRAISAL						
SAFETY		3	3			
GUEST COURTESY	3	3				
SHOW AWARENESS	3	3				

Another special project almost could be considered detached duty: we'd be pulled downstairs to the supervisor's office to help update (or write from scratch) the Standard Operating Procedures, or SOPs. Entire shifts would be taken up by the writing of outline-like procedures. Amazingly, we'd do this longhand, on notebook paper, and someone would later transcribe this using a typewriter. There weren't enough computers around to let us do it directly with a word processor, and this was before the dominance of the Microsoft Office software, anyway.

My time as Lead was marked by consistent attempts to reinvent our duties. I was always looking for new ways to do things, and especially new ways of squeezing out efficiencies. I experimented with crew meetings just before we opened the restaurant doors. That was, in part, an imitation of Roll Call, an event the managers around the park did every morning, to keep them informed of conditions specific to that day. After-hours meetings, after the doors were closed but before we cleaned up for the day, were also occasionally called. That was especially true if there were new policies or procedures about to be initiated, and these crew meetings provided the only venue for dissemination. But even then, they weren't very common.

Much more common were days that we would stay late and do extra cleaning. I take pride in being the person who invented this practice. On busy days where we'd made a lot of money, we could tell by predicting Sales Per Labor Hour (SPLH) and labor percentage of sales that the numbers would come in quite rosy for the day. In fact, we could forcibly extend everyone's shift at closing and still look great. With the supervisor's blessing, that's exactly what I would do. It wasn't always popular to extend shifts against the CMs' will, but it was something we were allowed to do according to the contract, so long as there was at least two hours' notice. This was a decision made somewhat early in the evening.

I'd had a somewhat eccentric algebra teacher in high school who, on some weeks, declared a "Turbo Tuesday," in which a lot of material would be introduced. I borrowed his language and called these late nights Turbo Closes. Turbo Closes worked like this: we'd do the regular nightly cleaning, during which I would wander about each station and take notes on what additional tasks could be done. Typically, Turbo Closes lasted an additional hour, and involved such things as dusting hard-to-reach places or applying brass polish to areas normally not touched. Any surface normally left alone during the nightly cleaning process was subject to being made bright and shiny during Turbo Closes.

People did complain about having to stay late for Turbo Closes unless they wanted more hours and more pay anyway. But the complaints were almost always half-hearted, and I sensed that usually there was a secret part of them that actually enjoyed the chance to merely clean, to make the place sparkle. I don't take credit for any of that. I think it had to do with Disneyland as a magical place. Here were workers, some of them quite jaded, who normally wouldn't admit to wanting to do much for Guests, but they were happy to be a part of making the magic happen, even in this small way. Management, of course, loved it. Our bottom-line numbers at the end of the day looked great, and the location received the equivalent of a miniature refurbishment at no additional cost.

As Leads, we had a lot of freedom to experiment with new methods. In fact, it was arguably part of the job description. We were charged with maximizing efficiency, and in a tray slide operation, that meant eliminating hold-ups as best we could. I championed a new position, a third person out on the serving line, where salads, desserts, and drinks were available, because, without a "third-line" person, the existing two had to leave their stations all the time to replenish food supplies. Management had not budgeted for this third-line position before, but it became part of the master schedule templates for busy days after a while.

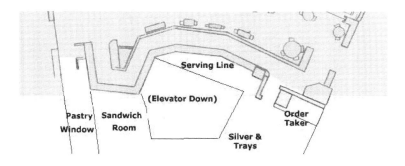

Another position I tried to roll out addressed slowdown at the order-take station. The order-taker was responsible for not just typing sandwich orders into the system, but also explaining how the system worked. On top of that, Guests didn't know what they wanted until they were asked to decide. My idea was to position someone standing ahead of the order-taker who would greet people, and that first person (I used the hybrid term greet-taker) would take the order onto little slips of paper. Then the order-taker would only need to take that paper and key the sandwich orders into the system. A good greet-taker would prevent any hold-up at the order-take station, and even if the greet-taker became the slowdown, he could skip a family or two and spread the order-taking load with the actual order-taker. It certainly generated additional sales by keeping the Guests in the trayslide moving constantly. The question was, did the extra sales generated justify extra hours? The answer we learned was that it helped only on busy days. If the greet-taker was so efficient there was no line left anymore, then precious seconds were lost in which there was no line at all, and the point of diminishing marginal returns for having the greet-taker was exceeded.

All of this experimenting with extra positions and maximizing the speed by which the Guests moved through

the line led to increased income. On New Year's Eve in 1994, we blew past the old daily sales record for the Café, helped in part by my experiments with extra positions, and we racked up a then-incredible $15,000 in net sales for the day from just our single location. When I was Lead at the French Market a few years later, similar experiments with additional positions led to breaking records there, too. Since the Market had essentially two lines (we called them Side A and Side B), it could reap more sales in a day. I helped break the record on a garden-variety August weekend in 1996, topping $22,000 in a single day from this one location.

Quite separate from the Lead's charge in general was the Empowerment Evolution of the mid-1990s, in which everyday, average hourly workers were encouraged to feel "empowered" to make decisions that guaranteed Guest happiness. In later years, this led to CMs giving away free items. For instance, if a Guest lost a balloon, any CM (and not just the Outdoor Vendors selling the balloons) was encouraged to feel empowered to get a new one for the Guest at no cost. They merely had to fill out a "no strings attached" form. This program originally started life as Total Guest Satisfaction (TGS). These changes were the result of the influx of new managers in the Team Disney Anaheim building, many of them holding MBA degrees, and full of concepts like "total quality response." Many old-time CMs wondered how their current mode of interaction with Guests was anything less than total quality! In many divisions of Disneyland, the end result of the Empowerment Evolution was the dissolution of the Working Leads positions, especially in Attractions. If the everyday CMs were empowered to do anything necessary, the reasoning went, then there was no need for Leads. This was seen in many quarters as an unmitigated disaster operationally to take away the Leads, and a few years later, they were re-instated. In restaurants, the Leads were never taken away, perhaps in an acknowledgement of their unique role.

To my mind, the ultimate expression of the Empowerment Evolution came a few years later, when Cathy, then manager of the French Market, decided that her restaurant was too hidden in the evenings, so she seized the initiative and created a work order to place deep-blue "Christmas" lights around the perimeter of her restaurant. It did the trick! The restaurant was visible from a distance and attracted a lot more attention, and thus more business. This was part of Cathy's plan—after all, by this time the "department" system had been replaced by a "business unit" system, which had the upshot of pitting restaurants in the area against each other for profit, rather than working together to provide a harmonious experience for Guests. Unfortunately for Cathy, her experiment proved short-lived, since it wasn't long until someone who worked at Walt Disney Imagineering noticed her little alteration. The folks at the Disneyland Design Studio were responsible for "Show Quality Standards," meaning that they decided what could go into the "show" and what could not, and they had not been consulted on Cathy's lights. They felt the advertising brought on by the lights was too much, and the effect distracted from the tranquil vista of New Orleans Square at night (the crowds massing for Fantasmic! kept it from feeling tranquil, but the lighting at least could be kept soothing). And so, a mere few weeks after the lights turned on, they disappeared again from the French Market.

Even before the Empowerment Evolution, CMs had always had the ability to alter their workplace, or at least to suggest changes. There was a suggestion box in each department—ours was outside the DEC—and the program went by the name I Have an Idea, complete with a Disneyfied logo: cute Mickey ears atop a light bulb. One dropped in a suggestion for altering the workplace, the idea being that workers on the ground have the best ideas about what to fix operationally, and if the idea was honored, the initiator would win $10, $25, or even $100 in Disney Dollars. And if the idea generated savings for the company, the initiator received a very tiny slice of it. My first suggestion was to install a rope next to the order-taker. For reasons no one understood at all, the wall forming the tray slide corridor did not start as Guests walked into the restaurant, so it was possible for Guests to wander into the dining room and not realize they just bypassed the place to order food. Meanwhile, the order-taker would have to call out, "Order over here, sir!" It was poor Guest service. They didn't want to install signs (that had been

a separate request of mine: install signs saying "order only sandwiches here") because signs encourage the worker to not talk with the Guest. But the lack of a rope always bothered me. My idea was turned down—no money for me—but I felt slightly vindicated when, years later, a rope was added after all. Not that I got any money from it.

In the sandwich room, we were constantly starved for space to store the sandwich ingredients. I suggested via I Have an Idea that we install pans at an angle from an overhead shelf, and we could put the lettuce in there, freeing up space for other ingredients in the middle. This idea was accepted, and I received not only the $25 reward, but a leather-bound calculator embossed with the I Have an Idea logo. Sadly, though, it was never implemented. The metal shop workers tasked with creating the new pan holders never followed through, though they did come out to make an initial assessment and spoke with me about the idea.

One final idea I had was honored with $100 and a framed certificate. I had noticed that Guests taking their trays past the final turn in the trayslide toward the cashier often ended up smashing their cheesecakes (and other desserts) into an overhanging lip some zealous woodcutter had left as a decoration alongside the trayslide. This resulted in many discarded desserts that had to be replaced. So I suggested shaving this overhanging lip flush with the wall, to avoid the ruined desserts. The wood shop guys showed up, verified what I wanted to do, and went to work. Since it was the end of my shift, I went home. When I returned the next day, I was greeted with the sight of the same overhanging lip as before, only now it took a gradual curve from the wall to achieve the lip. They hadn't solved anything at all—desserts would still be ruined. This problem was never addressed, and until the Café changed in 2006, the trayslide continued to have this problem.

Fortunately, most of the problems were operational in nature, and operational changes could fix things. When Fantasmic! began performances in 1992, the Café Orleans was the closest restaurant to "center stage" and people often tried to hold tables for hours on end, figuring they could get a good view of the show from here. We tried to convince them that by show time, the entire area between the water and them would be covered by people standing up, and the tables were not good spots. They were sometimes suspicious of our motives, thinking we only wanted the tables to seat more people. While that was true, we weren't lying about the view being no good. People who complained about us hounding them and stayed anyway were forced to stand up, the same as anybody else, once the show started, and CMs who were inclined toward revenge mirthfully noted the Guests' disgust.

We fell to patrolling tables and preventing any reserving of tables at all. We quickly discovered that asking folks to stand up and wait until their food arrived did not go over well, unless the policy was applied to everyone and the Guest was asked to stand within a few seconds of first sitting down. Squatter's rights seemed to set in otherwise. Bonnie was particularly good at persuading people to wait until their party had paid and was on the way out before sitting down, but this was always a negotiation.

About a year after Fantasmic! debuted, the esplanade area was refurbished to provide not only additional places to watch the show, but also established levels and higher grades. The net result was that the walkway directly in front of the Café was elevated, and people realized immediately that their view would be blocked and didn't even try to reserve tables. So the situation resolved itself.

But Fantasmic! was still a game-changer in our neck of the woods. Whereas previously our location had been quiet, and the area sleepy, once darkness set in, now we were very busy right up until 9:00, when the first show began. We experimented with staying open during that show, to pick up whatever business was left until the second show at 10:30, but there was usually very little demand, and eventually we'd close at 9:00 every night. That isn't to say there weren't attempts to cash in on Fantasmic! Early on, CMs Angela and Steve were sent out into the crowds, armed only with a money belt and a stadium-style carrier for drinks that could be reloaded with more sodas at the Pastry Window. It didn't catch on entirely, but the next idea did.

Kimberly, one of the Café Orleans assistant managers (by now we were calling supervisors "assistant managers"), came up with a plan to sell desserts in a prime viewing spot for Fantasmic!, namely, the balcony next to the Disney Gallery. Until this time, it had been a "first-come, first-served" kind of place. Visitors could simply line up at the staircase below, and at the appropriate hour, they were let up to the balcony, and the viewing was free. This spot was directly in the center of the show, as if Fantasmic! had been created to aim right at this particular point. Kimberly aimed to restrict the audience in this balcony to people who paid a premium, and she'd also set up desserts so they felt they'd paid for something besides the view. She tasked my friend Dawson to set up the operational details, and soon the Fantasmic Dessert Balcony was born. It originally cost a modest $20, but its runaway success led to numerous price increases. I worked the Fantasmic Dessert Balcony myself several times, and the fun of it was not only dressing up in a tuxedo, but in interacting with folks in an "all you can eat" environment, with the pressure off to maximize sales.

Here's what a typical day looked like:

16:00—Lead started work, picked up Ops Sheets and did the initial prep work.

18:00—Lead began to ready the balcony, recently emptied of the daytime visitors. A folding table was brought out, covered in a tablecloth, and the floral arrangements were set up. Silverware, plates, and cups were stocked below the table.

19:00—A second CM started work and assisted in the setup of the table. Hard-backed, padded chairs, such as those which can be found at most Disney food locations, were brought out to the balcony and arranged in two rows near the railings. Plenty of space was left between

the seats and the service table. In those early days, only
fifteen Guests per show were allowed on the Balcony.

19:50—Table was stocked with fresh fruit cuttings,
pastries, desserts, and silverware. Pitchers of mint julep,
water, and coffee were set nearby.

20:00—The first Guests arrived and were let in by Disney
Gallery personnel, who regulated the tickets and
reservations in the early days. Later, it would be taken
over by the Blue Bayou, and then by Guest Relations.
Much chit-chat ensued since there was little to do at
this point besides eat and talk.

21:00—First Fantasmic! performance. When the first
show ended at 21:22, Guests were encouraged to remain
for a few minutes, since the 21:30 fireworks were also
readily visible from their current location. Grateful, all
Guests resumed sitting, eating, and drinking.

21:45—Guests were warmly shown the door, as the next
set of Guests were waiting to be let in. Their show
started at 22:30, and they want to be pampered just as
much in advance of the performance.

In the early days, one great advantage of working these
shifts was the uniqueness of the costume. The Disney Gallery
CMs had a purple paisley vest, and the Blue Bayou CMs had
drab gray vests, but the Balcony CMs got to wear the tuxedoes
otherwise used only for certain private parties.

It wasn't that easy to worm my way into training on the
Balcony, since this was a location extremely heavy in Guest
interaction—my customer service skills had to be top-notch.
But the prestige was great, and for me, the ability to watch the
show with the Guests up on the Balcony was another fabulous
by-product. I never tired of that view.

When I wasn't working the Balcony, I was the night time
Lead at the Café. I had the seniority to request the day shift,
but I preferred evenings so I didn't have to wake up early. As

a consequence, I was around for almost every performance of Fantasmic! until 1997, when I left the company for a few years. I didn't watch every single second of every show, but I did hear it in the background, and to me it was infinitely better than the Main Street Electrical Parade, which frequently blocked my route back to Harbor House and had much more repetitive music. So ingrained was my Fantasmic! habit that, for a few weeks in 1997, when I found myself in Germany on unrelated business, I'd put on the Fantasmic! CD at 9:00, when it just felt right. When Disneyland announced that the 1,000[th] performance of Fantasmic! was at hand, I calculated that I had been present for at least 750 of them. No wonder I needed to hear that music at the appropriate time!

We're Not Carrots!

I worked in Department 959—New Orleans Restaurants—and our area manager Ray was quick to remind us that we were not to be called "New Orleans Foods." He often followed this reminder by exclaiming, "We're not carrots!" as if carrots and food were interchangeable in his mind. Because we were one big happy department, we did move around our group of restaurants sometimes, though we were hired into a particular restaurant or business unit.

At the Café we also worked in the Royal Street Veranda, and we manned La Petite Patisserie. Both of those window-service operations were about what one might expect. The Veranda was usually busy, and when it was not, we hoped the person who was working with us was interesting and knew how to sustain a conversation, or else the day would drag on. At the Pastry Window, business was almost always non-existent. And since one was working alone, one had spare time. Some Pastry workers were known to pop their heads above the saloon doors and take part in the conversations happening in the sandwich room.

More interesting were the times we were called into service at other locations in our department. The French Market was a recent addition into our department from Critter Country Restaurants, so they didn't exchange CMs all that often. There was a good amount of exchange with the Blue Bayou, though, especially when the Bayou needed bussers, or when we needed prep people. At the departmental level, letting people have an Early Release (or ER) was discouraged when any of our other locations was short-handed.

The Blue Bayou did not have any particularly grandiose Backstage areas. The bussers and servers worked out of server stations, the most interesting of which hid inside a fake cypress tree far off to one side. Its kitchen was unremarkable, and it did draw on the New Orleans Main Kitchen (NOMK) downstairs for some of its prep work.

It was quite common for the Cast cafeteria, the DEC, to be short on labor, possibly because working there was sometimes seen as odious, and turnover was pretty high. Thus, it was common for Café CMs to be pulled downstairs. We noted with some bitterness that this happened far less often to the Bayou CMs; never let it be said that a pecking order did not exist.

Working in the DEC (later re-named Westside Diner) was pretty simple: our fellow CMs would come and order sandwiches or dished-up meals. Working the grill was another matter; I had to learn various tricks for burgers and chicken. Happily, there was usually a fry-cook on hand. I noted with some irony that my pay rate at the Café was "Lead Fry Cook," which we were paid not because we had a fry-cook upstairs in the Café, but because it was the lowest-paying Lead rate for Foods under the contract.

One thing about being a Lead in the DEC that stuck with me was the different attitude toward money and productivity. If the target labor percentage for the Café was 17%, the target for the DEC was somewhere between 80% and 100%. The company was content to keep the prices low enough that it actually lost money on every transaction. The money coming in was enough to pay for the labor, but sometimes not the food costs (let alone the less-tangible costs, like their share of utilities bills). And forget profit.

Once in a while, we'd be pulled in to the NOMK, where an entire shift could be taken up making coleslaw or washing lettuce straight from the packing company. The NOMK was a big place. On the far side was Dry Storage, the main storeroom that, to my mind's eye, looked like a miniature Costco, though only one row wide. At one end of Dry Storage was the desk for the receiver, a person who sorted through all the deliveries to our location and kept the paperwork. In my early years, this was Paul, a seemingly grizzled man who appeared to have done this forever. On his desk was a nameplate that declared him the "Wise Old MKH." MKH was short for Main Kitchen Helper, which was then the term for someone who worked in the dishroom. So Paul was apparently an old-timer here who had risen through the ranks.

Most of NOMK was a series of long work tables, punctuated with deep sinks every so often, and a line of vats for soups and broths. This was all arranged in the center of the large room. Around the outside of this area were several walk-in refrigerators: A-box, B-box, etc., all the way up to I-box. Talk about massive food quantities! Walk into I-box and you'd find shelves all around the outside, and in the middle, a giant pallet of individual-sized milk containers, arranged in crates. To make sure nothing was left too long here, there were strict rules about rotation and taking the oldest ones: we took from the front, the top, and the left first, so when presented with a giant cube of crates like this, we started in the top-left corner. Newer stock would be rotated in at the opposite extreme (bottom right corner), and this ensured that nothing stayed on the pallet forever. I still use this method to this day at home with my more modest stores of things, like batteries.

Two sub-sections of the NOMK were especially lacking in people-power due to high turnover: the pot room and the dish room. The pot room took the hundreds of dirty pots and pans a busy department generates on a daily basis, power washed them, cleaned them with soap, dipped them in iodine, and returned the clean pots to a nearby room to be used again. There was something hot, repetitive, and odious about working here.

Not quite as bad was the dishroom. Here was the terminus of the conveyor belts from the Blue Bayou, French Market, and Café Orleans. A steady stream of full bustubs kept at least two people busy simply unpacking them, tossing away the trash, and loading the endlessly-cycling dishwasher with the dirty plates. The size of a large room, this dish machine was literally running all the time, save overnight, as giant racks of cups, plates, platters, and tumblers were endlessly loaded into it. On the other side, the dishes emerged clean, and someone had to remove them all and sort them into rolling containers that enabled easy re-stocking of the restaurants upstairs. This unloader had to be fast, and it was hard physical labor. On top of all that, the plates were hot to the touch; one often had burned fingers after such a shift, even wearing protective sanitary gloves. I could list a lot of negatives about working in the dishroom, but there was an upside: it was such physically demanding work and so consistently busy that the day seemed to go by very fast. Not fast enough for Hank, though, who one day started a rousing rendition of "99 Bottles of Beer on the Wall," making it all the way down to 38 before head chef Jules finally strode in and commanded them to shut up, since they could be heard throughout the NOMK.

The bustub conveyors traveled through tunnels cut in the concrete. Occasionally they would break, and a tub would get jammed up in the system. If that happened, someone had to jump in this canal, travel back to the point of the jam, and physically unblock it. We could do this for the Café Orleans conveyor, accessing the tunnel from the pot room, and every time I did it I marveled at the food and trash on the floor of the tunnel. No wonder rats were sometimes seen in the complex (more on that topic later), though I never encountered one in these tunnels. The Café conveyor merged with the Market's conveyor before reaching the dishroom, so that side was busier. The Bayou's conveyor was up in the ceiling. If a jam occurred here, CMs had to stand on ladders and lift ceiling panels in the DEC to get at the bustubs.

Our freezers were located out behind the building, in an open area bound by the Jungle Cruise on one side, the Disneyland Railroad berm on another (a tunnel for cars or people cut through that berm, giving us access to the Backstage road around Disneyland), and the Pirates of the Caribbean show building a third side. Before the Indiana Jones Adventure was built, the freezers sat right up against a wall that bordered on the Jungle Cruise. To one side was a doorway onto the On Stage area: this was the overflow queue for Pirates of the Caribbean, a long alleyway that cut deep into Backstage areas and alongside the Jungle Cruise. Later, that area became part of the Indiana Jones Adventure queue that was a long straightaway. Just before the bat cave was a set of tall doors on both sides of that queue—this was the truck access to the back side of the Jungle Cruise, right next to where our freezer used to be located.

We had other storage areas, too. The New Orleans Square complex was a multistory labyrinth, with the NOMK at the bottom and in the middle, and the restaurants arranged above it and on all sides. Zooming around and between all of that was the Pirates of the Caribbean ride—there were doors all down the main hallway toward the supervisor's office and the freezer out back, which were labeled as the areas of the ride, like the treasure room. Poke one's head into one of those unlocked doors, and one would see a scary maze of wooden two-by-fours, behind all of which were the On Stage portions of the ride. In the midst of all these restaurants and ride scenes was another store room, which we simply called by its numerical designation, 262. We'd store additional cups, cutlery, and plates in 262, so we'd be here to break out additional supplies if we found ourselves suddenly running low (which might also occur if the French Market managed to claim all the plates on a particular day). There was something intoxicating about an essentially limitless supply of plates. It didn't cost us anything. If we needed something, we simply went downstairs and got it.

And then there were the storage areas we seldom visited. We had a small storeroom with yet more equipment, needed only a few times per year, out in the old train station across the train tracks. Trivia buffs will note this was once used as the queue for the Frontierland train station, but now it is inaccessible. Its history is obvious when one is inside, though, for there are still framed photos on the walls. To get there, we had to cross the railroad track in full view of the Guests, and also make sure there was no train coming!

The final store room was intriguingly called the Cage. It turned out to be a sprawling set of caged-in areas individually padlocked, all located atop the French Market. We'd get there by ascending a winding staircase visible On Stage in the middle of New Orleans Square, but roped off to most Guests. At the top was a Backstage entrance to Club 33, the secret members-only club which took up most of the top floors in

New Orleans Square. Beside that was the Cage. All the restaurants had their own caged sections. This was more of a graveyard of equipment than a working storeroom, and we didn't need to come here often. The Club 33 folks were in this area all the time, though, since the Cage housed their walk-in refrigerator, and they used it to store all the wine they served. The entire area was originally going to be home to a jazz club, but these plans never advanced beyond the initial drawing board.

We found ourselves up on the third floor more often for a different reason: there was a bathroom up here used by Entertainment, which accorded a lot more privacy. Ostensibly all of our department was to use a bathroom down near the NOMK, opposite the chef's office. It held two urinals and one toilet—not enough for the whole population of workers! As CMs, we were not allowed to use the On Stage restrooms, though it was always amusing when a new-hire would do so anyway, not knowing any better. Instead, we'd use the Entertainment bathroom, part of a Backstage green room above the French Market and accessed by the same winding staircase we'd use for the Cage. Often, this area was completely empty. If it wasn't, we'd be subjected to stares by the entertainers, who undoubtedly must have been steamed at our temerity to come up and use their toilets. They had class, though: not once did they ever say anything to me, though in retrospect I would have understood fully if they had told us to get out and stay out.

Since we're on the subject of Backstage access points that are visible to On Stage Guests, I should mention the doors which led downstairs. Next to the Café was an unmarked door that opened up to a simple staircase. It rounded a corner and ended up near the bread aisle of the NOMK. At the end of that bread aisle was an elevator to the kitchen side of Club 33, located just to the side of the Disney Gallery. But that was the third floor. It also stopped on the second floor (i.e., ground level) and thus we called it the Veranda elevator. Once the elevator doors slid open, we had to open yet another door; this one swung out and so we had to do it slowly, lest a Guest be standing nearby unawares. This elevator hid in plain sight: the door was also unmarked, near a small hidden courtyard and basically opposite the entrance to Café Orleans.

On the other side of the land were the Guest restrooms, and here was yet another staircase leading to the Backstage areas, in this case, next to the DEC. One headed toward this Backstage door by following the path toward the men's bathroom for Guests, though, so it was always awkward for the women. Just inside the door, and next to the staircase, was yet another elevator. This was the freight elevator, which we hardly ever used unless the Veranda elevator was unavailable.

Every restaurant had its own elevator. The Bayou's elevator was opposite the DEC and opened on the second floor using the other side. This was also true of the French Market's elevator, which opened up near the dishroom and the side of the NOMK with fryers, which we called Hot Line. The Café's elevator was in the far side of the NOMK and opened on the same side at each floor. We also shared this elevator with Club 33, so we'd frequently be traveling partners. The Club folks had a reputation of one kind or another. The women were said to be "lifers" that never moved on to other jobs, because the tips were so good, and indeed there were numerous women in their thirties who did not look like the skimpy French maid's costume had been designed with them in mind. The men were said to be more effeminate than the general population—a charge also levied, with some justification, at the Entertainment department, particularly the parade performers. Sharing an elevator meant friendships were sometimes forged. One manager of the Club offered to let me make reservations at that exclusive eatery. "Any time you want," he declared magnanimously with a dismissive wave of his hand, as if it was no big deal for our two departments (they were a standalone department) to share favors. Naturally, I took him up on the offer and dined there with a friend on my birthday. In those early days, long before annual passholders were so numerous and the secret of Club 33 really was a secret, it probably wasn't a big deal after all. I'm not so sure it would be that easy for today's workers.

The Café elevator had a persistent bad odor. Water appeared to pool in the shaft below—no doubt due to carelessness on our part, when the door was open and we'd let liquid fall into the crack and down the shaft—and this water would turn rancid over time. To combat that, facilities workers would spray a highly pungent orange chemical into the shaft to mask the bad smell. I still recall the name: Formula 114. Later, when I visited EPCOT Center, I discovered that same odor in Horizons, on a set piece ostensibly showing the harvesting of oranges in the future. Apparently they use Formula 114 in the future!

The NOMK was our lifeline in the restaurants, and our dependence become all the more evident whenever the NOMK went down for annual refurbishment, usually timed to coincide with the yearly Blue Bayou and Pirates of the Caribbean downtimes. The Café would stay open, and we'd have to get all of our hot food, especially the clam chowder, from the main kitchen on Main Street, which served the Plaza Pavilion and the Tahitian Terrace (both of which were no longer restaurant locations by the time I ended my Disneyland service). We took an electric cart from the back door of our complex around to the Plaza Pavilion kitchen, and then retraced our steps back. It was a long process to get new food, and it slowed us immensely.

Annual refurbishments often meant a chance to not work for a week or more, though sometimes we were scheduled in locations that were new to us. During these downtimes, the location was given attention that was otherwise impossible during daily operation, such as re-painting, re-sanding, or replacement of equipment. There was a long list of things to be accomplished each year during rehabs, but seldom did all of it actually get done. Budgets, after all, were finite.

Apart from rehabs, we usually stayed within our department. On those days when we left the Café (or wherever our home location was), we were utilized within the area. On rare occasions we'd be cross-utilized at other food service locations around the park, especially in Hungry Bear Restaurant and the Bengal Barbecue. Since we were trained in Foods operations, this wasn't much of a stretch. It was both fun and taxing at the same time. Being in a new place generated excitement, but one never really felt at home, and one missed the camaraderie of the usual gang. In those days, Foods workers weren't tapped to help with parade and Guest control: that was the realm of the Attractions workers. The thought was that those workers were the most outgoing and social, and the ones most used to working directly with the public, so they were asked to do crowd control. By the mid-90s, this policy seemed to be abandoned, and restaurant workers also found themselves wearing the "bumblebee" outfit of Fantasmic! Guest control, or helping to steer Guests along the parade route. We'd come a long way from mere restaurant workers. Indeed, we certainly no longer were mere carrots!

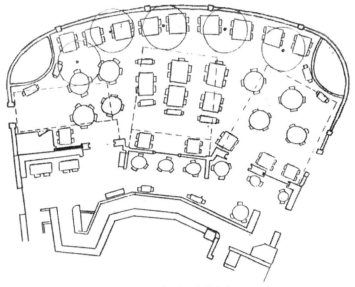

Seating diagram for the Café Orleans

Some Enchanted Evening

One of the company slogans prominently displayed in the Orientation booklets was "we work while others play." This could be interpreted as a philosophy, too, but mostly it was a policy, designed to ensure that new hires expected to be scheduled for special events, even those that fell outside of their normal availability.

The most oddball of my special assignments was the task to drive some tables out to Ray's house, where many of our managers were going to have some kind of company function. Ray was the area manager, responsible for all of Adv/Fr/NO/CC, and he had been with the park forever. His longevity was on ready display at his house, for he had three floor-to-ceiling display cases positively chock-full of buttons, ribbons, and pins from his years at Disneyland. Just looking at it was enough to generate a flutter of excitement. Years later, I'd see a display like this, though much smaller, at the Disneyland Hotel, and I'd think back to Ray's house.

Much more common were so-called "private parties" at Disneyland itself. In the 80s and early 90s, the park was commonly rented out on midweek evenings during the off-season, and since the whole park was re-opened for just the party Guests, it was expensive. Only the largest of corporations, with tons of employees to make happy, splurged on this expense. During private parties, the park operations were normal.

One variation of the private party concept dates all the way back to Walt's time (1961, to be precise): the Grad Nite. These were private parties that lasted overnight, and they offered scheduling difficulties for virtually all departments. We had to staff our normal operation and close down the day as usual, then bring in a second crew just for Grad Nite, but it couldn't be part of our normal crew, because they'd be needed again the very next morning. As a result, everyone was on the hook to work Grad Nites, even those who were in school and normally available only on weekends. One might imagine a lot of bleary-eyed grumbling, but most of the time, the workers didn't mind so much. It was fun to stay up all night, and the time usually went by quickly. In an effort to spread the joy, everyone was scheduled to work a few Grad Nites during the graduation season, so that no one was required to work every single one of them. Naturally, those who were high school students themselves didn't have to work on the night when their school was at Disneyland; they were allowed to request the day off, though they still had to pay to visit their Grad Nite, and they couldn't "sign in" for free that evening.

One reason the time passed quickly overnight was that the Guests were pumped full of energy. They were all young, of course, and they had been forced to dress up for the evening, so it felt like an important occasion. But most of all, they were excited because high school was over forever. Disneyland did its part to keep the energy high. There were special banners hung around key locations, there were dance stages set up (the French Market became a dance floor, too), and Disneyland actively courted the energy. Rock music, modern alternative, and even hip-hop was pumped in, not only at the dance floors, but it often replaced the usual Disney area music. It was a mind-bending experience to walk down Main Street and hear thumping tunes with lyrics that would have made Walt blush.

All that energy could have led to rowdiness, of course, but we saw no shenanigans in the Café Orleans. I imagine the Attractions CMs had a harder time of it. Certainly Security had to take special measures, as the Guests were visually frisked before they were allowed On Stage—bottles and alcohol were a perennial problem. The high school grads arrived by bus, and those busses ate up enormous amounts of room in the Cast parking lots. The kids would be escorted Backstage, behind Space Mountain, in a staging area before the park was cleared of the day Guests. A sea of cones helped them stay away from the working areas of Backstage.

One further variation of the private party concept was the company-hosted private party. I'm thinking primarily of one specific event: the retirement party for a Disneyland executive named Jack Lindquist. Jack had been Disneyland's first president (before him, there had only been vice presidents), and when he retired in 1993, management threw him a big party located in his crowning achievement—the recently opened Mickey's Toontown. The best and brightest CMs from around the park were called upon to work this event, and I was tapped to work one of the food tables.

At the event itself, which was confined to Mickey's Toontown, the atmosphere was rendered festive by balloons attached everywhere, special colored area lighting rigged in the trees and atop buildings, and all the usual tables set up to service the visitors. Those tables included an open bar, so many Guests got sloshed. I can vividly recall hearing a well-known drunken restaurant executive slur his words while trying, and mostly failing, to hold a conversation.

During the celebration, Disney executives celebrated Lindquist's departure by presenting him with a 23-foot boat, since he enjoyed fishing so much. The boat was tiny and lifted aloft by a crane for dramatic effect. During the ceremony, however, a horrendous "accident" occurred, and the boat was dropped onto the ground and smashed. We were in on the joke, though, and we knew this was an orchestrated accident to engage Lindquist in one final bit of frivolity. His real boat rested Backstage, unbroken (and considerably larger). Lindquist was later commemorated at Disneyland with the form of an artificial pumpkin in his likeness—complete with eyeglasses—located in Toontown.

Lindquist's party was attended by many Hollywood stars. When one works at Disneyland, one gets used to seeing celebrities every so often, though at the Café this was less common than most other locations. I once helped then-mayor Sonny Bono carry a tray to his table. A different time, when I saw that actor Wil Wheaton (Star Trek's Wesley Crusher) was in the building, I approached him to chat about a mutual friend. Mostly, though, we saw celebrities and didn't say anything to them (selling coffee to Kurt Russell leaps to mind). Being left alone is what they wanted, especially if they were traveling without an entourage and without a Disneyland Guest Relations host. When we saw Paula Abdul at the Pastry Window (Roxanne was delirious that she got to serve her), she was with a Guest Relations hostess, presumably to be granted backdoor access to the rides. Disneyland agreed to escort famous people around only if denying such a move would mean too much disruption from the paying public mobbing the star. Thus, backdoor access was especially granted to the big stars, which in the early 90s included Michael Jackson. Jackson always traveled around Backstage and popped up On Stage only at the last second. His entrance to the Blue Bayou, for instance, took him through our hallways and up stairs to an arcane back door, and he'd cross a bridge over the Pirates of the Caribbean boats to get access to the Blue Bayou tables. The whole restaurant would eventually be smothered in whispers, but people left him alone.

Although the stars crossed our path sometimes in the Café, these private parties really upped the stakes as to how many celebrities we'd see at once. At Lindquist's party in Toontown, I spent several minutes chatting with Robin Williams, who was disarmingly toting around infant child Zelda in a backpack. Other celebrities I saw that night included Candice

Bergen, Tony Danza, Danny DeVito, Roy Disney, Jr., Michael Eisner, Sally Field, Whoopi Goldberg, John Goodman, George Lucas, Tom Selleck, Sinbad, Steven Spielberg, and Damon Wayans.

As much fun as Lindquist's goodbye party had been, the private parties that stick out the most in my mind were the Enchanted Evenings. These were like private parties where an external company rented the whole park, except that Enchanted Evenings were restricted to just one land to keep the cost down. The visitors only rented a small slice of Disneyland. They sometimes chose Adventureland or Fantasyland, but usually the choice was New Orleans Square, home to favorite attractions Haunted Mansion and the Pirates of the Caribbean. After its introduction in 1992, Fantasmic! was often included as well.

For Enchanted Evenings, which typically ran on weekday nights until shortly after midnight, the area was dressed to the nines. Giant bundles of tightly-wound balloons arranged in a long line were curved across the Pirates bridge, forming arches of balloons that created an entryway to the party. The arches were internally illuminated, rendering the look that much more magical. Trees and buildings were rigged with special lights that gave the ground color, designs, and motion. Music filled the area, often Disney music, in a land that normally lacks a loud soundtrack, making it extra special. We CMs were also dressed up: we wore tuxedoes (a special issue from Costuming), which added excitement on our end. Companies that rented part of the park for an Enchanted Evening paid a lot of money, so the expectation that we would serve every last person with kid gloves, and deference was quite high.

During an Enchanted Evening, the regular restaurants were closed, and food was served instead from tables set up out in the esplanade. Decked out with expensive linens and skirting, and usually sporting a rich or even ostentatious centerpiece, the table display consisted of a Y-shape of several banquet tables in a row which formed two serving lines. We'd set up chafing dishes heated by Sterno flames below. Best of all, our menu was quite different for these events. We served our spicy chicken dish (the Café's Poulet de la Maison), mouth-watering Swedish meatballs on noodles, and a tangy seafood combination. Runners obtaining food from downstairs to restock the tables were known to pry open the pans and snack on the tasty food in the elevator, though this was by no means condoned.

In addition to food tables, we had open bars, where the liquor was free to the Guests. CMs had to be 21 to work these bar tables, and one of my favorite jobs was to be the Bar Boss, the coordinator of all the bars at the Enchanted Evening. I was accused of liking this job so much because it entailed wearing a radio and earpiece, something we don't normally do at the Café, and I can't deny that that was part of the allure. Of course, not everything was glamorous for a Bar Boss. I'll never forget when two underage female television stars came to the bar looking for drinks. Since they were so famous, I recognized them on sight and even knew exactly how old they were, and told them we were very sorry, but we couldn't serve them. They grew quite petulant at this treatment and even called us some names, though, of course, they did not have IDs with them to prove their ages; they wanted to trade on their fame for the alcohol. I recall seeing them later with drinks in their hands—apparently a friend or handler had obtained drinks for them.

One night, fellow CM Julie and I were given round trays full of champagne flutes to carry out to Guests as they arrived via Disneyland Railroad, and she insisted on adding more and more flutes to her tray. Any waiter will know that she was bound to unbalance herself, particularly if she tried to hold the tray with just one hand, which, of course she did, in an attempt to look debonair. The tray crashed to the ground, sending glass and alcohol flying, just as the train pulled in. We were slightly hidden behind the French Market, so we had to scramble to clean up, and we barely made it before the first visitors reached our line of sight.

Most Enchanted Evenings were fun to work and largely uneventful. Even before Fantasmic!, we sometimes got to see fireworks on the river stage—part of me wonders if this is where the idea for Fantasmic! first took form. Those fireworks on the river stage, though, were jury-rigged, so they weren't quite as safe. I watched with a mixture of fascination and horror as one rocket shell launched straight for the Haunted Mansion and landed in the grass next to it, starting a small fire which quickly brought the fire department. Smaller fires on the stage itself were even more common.

When the last Guest for the evening had left, we'd begin cleaning up and breaking down all the tables. One food table was left deliberately in full working order, however, for management always allowed us to eat the leftover food here when we were done with everything else. This was a tremendous perk, and a very unusual one, considering the normal rules about not eating company food. But it was done as a thank-you to the Cast for making the evening perfect for the visitors, and also as a way to express gratitude that people would work this evening shift, when normally they wouldn't be available.

The granddaddy of all Enchanted Evenings was the birthday party for Elizabeth Taylor. As she was turning 60, she wanted to throw a gigantic party for herself, so she rented all of Fantasyland and staged a lavish affair much like the other Enchanted Evenings. We were all in tuxes, the area was specially lit, and the balloon chains this time went straight up into the air rather than forming arches. Liz's table was atop a raised area next to Dumbo, and my drink table was positioned just in front of Dumbo.

Actually, it wasn't my table at all; it was Dale's. Dale was a fellow Lead from the Café and more senior than I, so it made sense that he would be the Table Lead. Yet, for whatever reason, I felt betrayed. When asked if I'd like to work this event, I'd been asked to be the Table Lead, so I said yes. Leads often don't like to work non-Lead shifts. Once they've made the transition, many don't like to return to "peon" duties (Disneylander language is nothing if not crass). Looking back on it now, it seems childish that I should have cared, but I mentioned it to my immediate manager while we were setting up for the party, and her boss, an area manager named Roberta, later told her to "get him out of here" as they couldn't risk having a sourpuss around once the party started. She was absolutely right, too. My manager came back to me and reported what Roberta had said but didn't send me home, asking instead if I could work a non-Lead shift and still be happy to be here. I came around immediately, of course—who knows what I'd been eating that day to give me such a sense of entitlement—but I was able to make the attitude adjustment readily enough.

I was glad that I did, for the event was historic. Liz Taylor was big news then, and three paparazzi helicopters circled over Fantasyland, hoping to snap pictures of the party. I saw still more celebrities and had a very long talk with Henry Winkler (who played "the Fonz" in *Happy Days*), a real down-to-earth guy. The key to interacting with celebrities is to talk about whatever they want, not to ask questions they field from fans all the time. Of course, the seeking of autographs is strictly prohibited. The one celebrity I'd wanted to meet, Arnold Schwarzenegger, was supposedly there but I never encountered him. I spoke German, so I looked forward to conversing with him in his mother tongue, but sadly I never got the chance. It seems that, even on Enchanted Evenings, not every wish comes true.

Maggots, Fires, and Falling Elevators

Murphy's Law is known to everyone, and even in Walt's Magic Kingdom, not everything went according to plan. It might be more accurate to say the exact opposite; that things went wrong all the time. Even in my own tiny little restaurant, there were accidents, slips and falls, minor injuries, and almost routine equipment failures.

We had heavy floor mats in the kitchen areas of our restaurant to prevent slips, though, of course, at the end of the night, when the mats were lifted away, the accumulated spills made the ground doubly treacherous, and slips were common. More dangerous was the highly slick tile in the indoor dining area of the Café. Any moisture at all turned this region into a danger zone. Guest slips were uncommon, thank goodness, but CM slips did occur. One comical fall that sticks in memory occurred when a pre-opening meeting was to take place in the dining area. Most of us had gathered there, but laggard John was just rounding the doorway from Pastry Window and coming up on the cashier station, when he slipped on ice and plopped down on his rear. Uninjured but embarrassed, he endured a lot of ribbing for this feat. Making fun of someone else (good-natured and occasionally otherwise) was a way of life at Disneyland, and entirely to be expected. It was part of the culture.

More sinister slips occurred as well. The Café offered a refill station for hot water, coffee, decaf, and iced tea out in the indoor dining room, and those containers had to be replaced manually every so often. The iced tea was the only one not plugged in to a heater, but the heat from the others accidentally led to this liquid becoming too hot, and people sometimes dumped the warm tea into the spill tray below. Likewise, the poorly-labeled pots led people to pour hot water when they were looking for coffee, and this, too, would fill up the spill trays. The trouble was, those spill trays didn't drain anywhere; they just overflowed down the table and onto the slick tile. So heading out to the refill cart could be dangerous, especially if one was carrying a metal container of fresh, hot coffee. Poor Annie learned this first-hand. She slipped on that liquid pooled on the floor, and the scalding coffee spilled from the refill container onto her hands and arms. Her burns were not extensive, thankfully, but she did get transported to Central First Aid (CFA) and later went home.

When CFA was called, usually via the non-emergency number, they would come out to the location to investigate. A nurse was dispatched from CFA (or from Critter Country, on very busy days, when an ancillary First Aid office was open), and the nurse would always bring along a wheelchair. She was also accompanied by a Security officer. Meanwhile, all park pagers and radios would crackle with the news that there was a "CFA run" and the location would be named. Codes were used so as to not alarm the population who might overhear the radios. A "Code One" indicated a routine medical problem, and a "Code Two" implied something a lot more serious, usually with the city paramedics coming On Stage. Show and theme were being broken to ensure the safety of someone. "Code Three" was a life-or-death warning, and when those were issued, supervisors from all over the park sprinted to get there. I must have called CFA out several times over the years, always Code One, except for one Guest who had heart pain— Security upgraded his call to Code Two pretty quickly. Annie, with her coffee burns, was a Code One, and for some reason, the nurse insisted she ride back to CFA in the wheelchair, even though she could walk just fine. Annie found it humiliating, she told me later, and indeed, I'd seen other CMs in wheelchairs over the years who actually covered up their faces as they made their way through the On Stage crowd.

Not every accident led to a CFA run; I saw first-hand how one instead led to a written reprimand. While cutting croissant sandwiches, I saw that the large, serrated bread knife I was using was separating from its handle, so I wanted to throw the old one away. In a misguided attempt to stay at my post and maximize production, I stupidly just tossed the old knife toward a trashcan at the back of the room, perhaps four feet away from me. There was no one between me and the trash, so it seemed to be safe. But I had been standing in a spot

that was surrounded by several blind corners. As bad luck would have it, Shawna rounded the corner at exactly the wrong moment, and my flying knife nicked her wrist and bounced away. Horrified, I apologized, and while Shawna understood my reasons, she still had to

report it, and I got a written reprimand as a result. Amused, my fellow co-workers teased that I had been aiming at her the whole time. One of them even drew a cartoon lampooning the event.

But accidents weren't the only things to go wrong; pests and vermin cropped up from time to time also. There are plenty of feral cats at Disneyland, usually quite hidden from the visiting Guests because they only come out at night, and the abundance of cats suggests there are plenty of rats and mice to hunt. One wholly unsubstantiated theory purports that these cats are descendants of the felines kicked out of Sleeping Beauty Castle when Walt wanted a display installed in that space, which was then unused.

Mice weren't a big problem in our restaurant. We had glue traps occasionally, and I can only recall one time when we caught one. Oddly, the department we were supposed to call when a live animal was trapped was Landscaping. They came out and took away whatever had been caught, presumably to destroy it.

Rats were another story. We had those. We were never quite sure where they lived; presumably, behind the woodwork of the ornate (and, by then, twenty-year-old) serving line. They were quite dormant during the day, and when the place would bustle with activity at closing, they were not to be found. But after things quieted down, it was a pretty certain thing they'd come scurrying out. Sightings were not made daily or even weekly, but they were common enough that each one caused only a mild rush of interest.

On the serving line, we had a warmer that normally stayed deeply set into the woodwork. On rare occasions, we'd pull the warmer out and see numerous rat droppings atop it, implying the rats called the woodwork home. There was a crawlspace in the wood which connected the line and the sandwich room. Only Trent was brave enough to navigate this scary space which was surely rodent-infested.

Undoubtedly the entire New Orleans Square area had rats in the infrastructure. At the French Market, where I later worked, there was a giant fake skylight in the ceiling, illuminated not by the sun but by fluorescent lights above. I once watched from below as a rat crossed this glass, his figure clearly illuminated by the lights above it, and his long tail marking him as a rat. I could hardly believe my eyes, though, for he was almost the size of a cat, and except for that dragging tail, I might have doubted myself. But the shape was certainly that of a vermin, and the enormous size merely confirmed my opinion that these creatures were omnipresent. The worst part was that this incident occurred in the middle of the dinner rush, and Guests were all around. Thankfully, none looked up and saw what I had seen.

We weren't so lucky with another pest problem in the Market. It started with Guests noticing little things dropping into their soda glasses as they stood in the trayslide, and then they took a closer look. They were maggots, squirming and alive. The problem was quickly isolated: the air-conditioning vents, long lines cut into wooden beams in the ceiling, were dropping maggots onto the food, into drinks, and even onto people's hair. Presumably, maggot larvae had been laid in the air conditioner unit itself, which would have to be cleaned thoroughly. The Market closed for the day, of course, and we Café Orleans denizens found this unfortunate turn of events for our rivals to be deliciously funny, and we renamed the restaurant the "French Maggot." Apparently some of the Market inhabitants had a sense of humor about it, too. When I rehired into the Market a couple years later, someone showed me a spot On Stage but facing away from Guests that had small bits of graffiti, one of them a Liquid Paper scrawl of the words "French Maggot" and the date of the incident.

Equipment failed all the time. It seemed like our ice machine broke down more often than anything else, but at least we could get ice from other locations. One piece of critical hardware, our elevator, broke down at least once a year. We'd be forced to use the Veranda elevator and then take the food (or clean plates, or whatever was being brought upstairs) out On Stage and cross the street to get to the Café kitchen. Food had to be covered when exposed to the outside world like that, but the cover was a good thing anyway, because that street was laid with cobblestones, and whatever cart we brought with us rattled around so much that spills were likely. Clam chowder had to be brought from downstairs into the Veranda in this fashion all the time anyway, since the Veranda elevator didn't actually go to the Veranda. Folks quickly learned to not overfill the chowder pot, lest it spill all over the cart full of fritters we were bringing.

The cobblestones presented another problem. The carts we were bringing across the street sometimes caught on the uneven surface and overturned, which was especially likely if they were top-heavy. I've seen a fritter cart go down like this. The fritter cart was a seven-foot tall enclosed box on wheels, the size of a wardrobe, and it contained sheet pans full of pre-made fritters and sometimes also pots of steaming chowder resting on the bottom. If one of those fell down on a child, it was heavy enough to do real damage, perhaps even cause a death. I once had to catch a cart already leaning over before it could hit a passing boy.

The worst, though, were the flat-bottomed carts we used to collect the dirty trays and silverware, and later for returning the clean trays and silverware back upstairs. The stack of trays was precarious and top-heavy just by itself, since it was freestanding on the cart. But then we put racks of silverware atop that, which dangled off one side because the racks were longer than the trays. Normally, this was all invisible to Guests, but if the elevator broke, we'd have to venture outside to find another elevator. Once I was using the freight elevator near the On Stage restrooms to transport silver and trays when my wheels caught on something, and the entire column fell over into the street. Fortunately, these were all clean—I was returning to the Café, not coming from it—but that didn't make the noise any less loud. KER-PLAM! The smack of hard plastic trays on the stone street would have been resoundingly loud, even if it didn't echo off buildings on both sides of the narrow street. The clean silverware scattered and clattered. Worst of all, it was a crowded day, and the falling objects narrowly missed several people. One Guest with quick reflexes jumped as the wave of trays roared at him; he might well have been knocked over by it otherwise. After the fall, there was shocked silence from the Guests, who all stopped and looked at me, their mouths agape, as if they couldn't comprehend something like this happening at Disneyland. I looked at them, and they still didn't react. To fill the silence, and not knowing what else to do, I held out my arms wide and questioningly, and asked, "Isn't anyone going to clap?" That broke the spell, and they did clap and laugh, and many helped me restack the trays, which now had to be brought downstairs again, to be rewashed, meaning still more trips in the borrowed elevator.

If the elevator broke down with people inside it, there was an unspoken rule that CMs could simply help themselves to the food they were traveling with (if they were bringing stock up to the Café) without fear of reprisal. After all, they were trapped. Once it broke down with Helen inside, who was stuck for a good two hours. We pried open the door on our level and ascertained we could see into the elevator cab: it had descended somewhat from our level, but a few inches were still overlapping with our space. Since she was thirsty, we rigged together a series of straws and poured Coca-Cola down to her. That was a bit messy, as one might readily imagine, not so much from any leaks in the makeshift pipeline, as from the forcing of liquid via gravity. When Helen took the straw out of her mouth, soda kept pouring out, some of it onto her costume.

Not too long after that event, I was ascending to the second floor when the elevator made a series of vertical jerks as it neared our floor. That was frightening, so as I got out, I told the people waiting to go down to stand by for a minute, and I sent the elevator down alone. After a few seconds, a resounding boom and crash made everyone in the restaurant aware there was a problem. We pried open the door and peered down. The elevator had turned partly sideways and two of the walls had fallen inward. Had I gone down, I might have been crushed. We got a new elevator after that, at a cost of $36,000.

I associate the elevator with one more story. My friend Dale, a fellow Lead, was taking recalcitrant CM Tim down to the supervisors. "Let's go, now! In the elevator!" Dale had shouted to Tim. Dale later confided to me that Tim had gotten in his face the whole way down, saying nothing but staring hard at him, a mere few inches away, as if contemplating how much trouble he'd get in for punching Dale. This resonated with me, since I wondered how I might react if I had to bring someone downstairs to meet with the supervisors. Would I have Dale's conviction? Was it my job to take a punch to the jaw? Apparently Dale worried about the same thing, because shortly after this incident, he started working out and soon sported muscular arms, quite a transformation from his previous thin frame.

I can't say that violence erupted much among our Cast, though perhaps it was part of the make-up of our Cast. During the L.A. riots of 1992, we employed some folks who lived in the affected areas who either drove that long distance themselves, or were bussed in. We nervously reported to work one day, worried that the spreading violence was about to poke into Orange County, and wondering what might happen at Disneyland. One rough-looking guy named Tony (who was a friend and would be a great guy to have on your side in a dispute) lived out there. I asked him on that day if he'd seen any violence. Sure, he said. But had he taken part in any himself? He grinned in a manner that was either sheepish or mischievous, or both, and said his friend had broken a storefront window, so he picked up a brick and re-broke the same window. I'm not convinced I got the whole story from him. Fortunately, that day was the closest the L.A. riots got to Disneyland.

Drugs were more common than violence. CMs who were hung over were not chastised; in some ways, it was almost expected. We weren't supposed to be at work drunk or on drugs, of course, though I know of someone who took pride in being stoned at work as often as he could be. A worker from the DEC was allegedly caught smoking marijuana in the Cast parking lot and terminated on the spot. He was the only CM I know of who lost his job due to drug use.

Theft was another matter. People did lose their jobs to that. I was once walking through the Backstage area between Frontierland and Adventureland, and ahead of me was a contingent of supervisors and Disneyland Security officers, escorting a girl in a River Belle Terrace costume. She was agitated, loudly protesting her innocence, and gesticulating wildly. One of her wild arm swings inconspicuously launched a small object to the side that had been concealed in her palm. I saw it only because I was behind this whole posse. Unfortunately for the River Belle CM, one of the Security guards saw it too, picked it up, and unfolded it to expose two tightly packed $100 bills. I surmised this worker had been accused of stealing from her cash drawer and had been trying to ditch the evidence, only she got caught at it. I watched all this, bemused, and recalled that it had also been a River Belle girl I had seen one previous summer performing the worst violation of the Disney Show I'd ever witnessed. She sat down at the entrance to Adventureland in costume and smoked a cigarette, right there amid the Guests.

But stealing certainly happened in our department as well. When I first started in 1987, individual cashiers were trained to stop at Cash Control at the beginning of their shift, and they'd pick up their own funds individually. As each cashier left, he simply slung the burlap cash bag over his shoulders and made his way across the park. The switchover to cash carts began in the early 1990s. Scuttlebutt has it that a cashier from the Blue Bayou claimed to have been robbed right there in the park, as she brought her cash fund at the end of the day (stuffed with the day's receipts, not just the $300 start-up money) back toward Cash Control, though the same rumors suggested park management didn't quite think she was completely innocent in the robbery. Regardless, New Orleans Restaurants was the very first department to get a cash cart, so it seems likely that we did precipitate the trend that would become universal. From that point on, only Leads would check out money and return it at the end of the day.

If not using a locked cash cart, we were required to shove the distinctive burlap money bag into a Disneyland merchandise bag, as though we'd just purchased a souvenir. I always marveled at how easily one could see through this. Near shift-change times in late afternoon, any CM seen strolling toward Tomorrowland, with a Disneyland merchandise bag slung over his shoulder, was obviously a cashier returning money. A determined theft would still have found cashiers an easy mark.

Having a cash cart was probably a wise precaution. I know of several cashiers who were terminated for stealing. Especially with our old Point of Sale (POS) computers, it was possible to simply ring up the total, tell the Guest the total, and then instead of finalizing the sale, push a button to cancel the transaction, another button to open the drawer (the "No

Sale" button), and then manually provide the correct change so the Guest would be no wiser. Of course, there would also be no receipt.

This method of theft was employed by one CM in the Veranda on a particularly busy day, with perhaps $80 worth of sales withheld from the computer and thus not calculated. The act ruined what would otherwise have been a record-breaking day in the Veranda, which missed cresting the $10,000 mark in a single day by only $30.

Eventually, that loophole was closed so that no one could push the "no sale" button, yet still there was theft. A supervisor once asked us Leads to tally up the ways we could imagine someone could steal. I came up with seven ways, and I imagine they used our information to search the records of the transactions and find additional thievery.

Sometimes they needed that evidence, and sometimes they didn't. There were "secret shoppers" around that would visit locations and grade them on everything from speed and efficiency to smiles and pleasantries. They'd watch for a suspicious lack of receipts, too.

I was once visited by the ultimate in secret shoppers, the CEO himself. In 1988, fairly early in Michael Eisner's term, he came through the Café Orleans serving line in disguise and all by himself. I wasn't fooled by his baseball cap, though, and knew right away who he was. I didn't let on, however, and simply treated him with the same respect as any other Guest. We must have done well, since we didn't hear back about any problems.

Security had a sub-branch of their force working in plain clothes, called Fox units. Fox units prowled the park, watching for stealing from Guests and CMs alike. They were notoriously hard to spot at restaurants, though I found them easy to locate as they shadowed people in shops, especially on Main Street.

Mainly, though, managers and Security had only suspicions, not evidence. So they relied on other tactics to wrangle confessions out of people. Many would call them "trick confessions," or even badgering. Linda was once hauled off for half her shift and accused multiple times of having stolen. She never admitted to it. She knew there had been instances in the past where Security got people to admit they had stolen *something*, perhaps not money, but maybe a single bite of bread, and even that small admission was enough to get one terminated. It was almost as though they had selected someone for termination, and the exact method was merely a formality. As Linda continued her denials, her interrogators from Security brought out the big guns. We have video, they told her, and she promptly demanded to see it, since she knew there were no video cameras installed at the Veranda, where she had been working. Eventually they let her go, and the cloud of suspicion wafted away. Linda may have been caught up in a tattletale-ring, whereby Security promised one CM who had admitted stealing that criminal charges wouldn't be filed if he named other stealers. Who knows how reliable this method was for obtaining actionable intelligence?

Disney took stealing quite seriously. One time I wore home the belt that had been issued to me as part of my Lead costume, since my street clothes were just a touch too baggy for an event I wanted to attend after work. While hanging out at Harbor House waiting for some other CMs to get off work, I spoke casually with the Security officer there, and when he noticed the belt buckle, he was sharp enough to know it was a Disneyland belt. He asked me about it, and of course I told him the truth, after which the entire event snowballed quickly. SAM-1 (the person in charge of all of Security at Disneyland for the day; a rotating position) had to come out to talk to me and take my statement. My own managers were notified. As Leslie (my manager at the time) noted, this was a pretty stupid thing for me to do. Even though the costume was issued to me and I was still on the hook for returning all the pieces, it was considered stealing because I had taken it beyond Harbor House. This was, naturally, in the days before FastTrack. I got a written reprimand on my record as a result.

Though I didn't need the help for this one infraction, I could have turned to the union for assistance, had my job been in jeopardy. The vast majority of workers at Disneyland are part of a union, and it was required that we join if we wanted the job. We were part of Hotel Employees and Restaurant Employees (HERE) Local 681, consisting mostly of Disneyland restaurant employees and those working at all branches of the Disneyland Hotel. Union dues automatically were taken from my paycheck, though they were only a few dollars and the dues were not taken out of every paycheck.

Disneyland 1313 Harbor Boulevard, Anaheim, CA 92803			ORD DY/WKY OP						C955166		627115
Employee Name			Social Security No.	Origin	Dept.	Location	WS	Pay Period	Week Ending		
KEVIN YEE				02	959	652	03	40	09/29/90		
									BATCH 0015		

Computation of Gross			Miscellaneous Deductions		Taxes	
Description	Hours	Earnings	CREDIT UNION	50.00	Federal Income	17.51
STRAIGHT TIME	18.2	168.08			Federal Insurance Contribution Act	13.71
OVERTIME	.8	11.08			State Disability Insurance	1.62
					State Income CA	.95
					City Income	
					Total:	33.79
					Year To Date Totals	
					Gross	10247.46
					Federal Income Tax	1179.35
					Federal Insurance Contribution Act	783.93
Total Gross:	19.0	179.16			State Disability Insurance	92.23
Total Deductions & Taxes:		83.79			State Income Tax	166.88
Net Pay:		95.37	Weekly Total	50.00	City Income Tax	

The union handled collective bargaining, but it wasn't an equal playing field. There was heavy bias to adjust the contract to favor longtime workers, not the new hires, because only the "dinosaurs" showed up to union meetings and to vote. But the union served another purpose: they got people their jobs back if they had been fired unfairly.

In some cases, they got the jobs back for people who should probably have stayed fired. Jonathan, one of our most problematic workers who engendered lots of Guest complaints for rudeness, always teetered on the brink of termination (later, the euphemism "forced separation" was created) not only for those written complaints against him, but also for his own attendance problems. Somehow he always managed to cling to his job, often with heavy assistance from the union.

Yet, as much as Jonathan provided a steady stream of headaches, he was at least predictable in some ways. It was when things went wrong that were unusual and unpredictable that one started to worry. As far as unusual goes, what sticks out most in my mind is the day our manager Leslie called me downstairs to the office and informed me in undertones that there had been a bomb threat called in to Disneyland—this was many years before 9/11—and would I please go back to my location and look around for a bomb? She assured me our area had not been specifically mentioned—this precaution of looking around was happening all around the park. So I went back upstairs and beat around the bushes—there weren't many shrubs around the Café—and of course found nothing. Nor did anyone else that day; it apparently was a prank. But I always found it odd that the rank-and-file should be mobilized to look for bombs.

Phantom bombs may conjure up visions of conflagration, but at least they are imaginary. Real fires that began from more mundane sources of ignition were far more common. We were told at Orientation that trashcan fires sometimes occurred because people would place still-smoldering cigarette butts into the trashcan. A simple method was suggested to resolve the situation. Just shake the trashcan violently, we were told, and often the nascent fire would be extinguished. The idea was that leftover soft drinks and ice in the trash would be shaken out of their cups and onto the fire. Clearly that worked better in the days before lids were placed on every soda cup! If the trash stopped smoking, we didn't need to sound a frantic alarm. We still had to phone the fire marshal, but he didn't need to rush out. Calling in a live fire would bring the fire marshal, as well as numerous managers from around the park, on the double.

I got to call in only one live fire during my time, but one was enough. I was at the Lead desk in the Café when Margie reported billowing smoke coming out of the Hatco warmer in Pastry Window, a heater we used to keep extra stock of the nighttime entrees for the sandwich room. I took one look and saw gray smoke rapidly curling up the wooden frame—the entire drink and warmers assembly was covered over by wooden panels to present an ornate appearance, and the presence of all this wood worried me greatly.

After one look, my brain made an instantaneous switch to crisis mode. It wasn't panic by any means; rather, decisions were made quickly, calmly, and rationally, though I suspect in this mode I wouldn't have brooked much argument from my co-workers. First, I called Central Communications (it didn't occur to me until later that I missed my only chance to call the Disneyland 911) and told them I had an apparent electrical fire (it also didn't occur to me until later that I missed my chance to show off that I knew the radio code, which was 904). These missed opportunities didn't cross my mind at the time; I was in chess mode, thinking three or four steps ahead. I also paged my manager on duty, leaving a voice message to have him call me.

I grabbed my Ops sheet. I knew that in the event of an evacuation, I'd have to account for all my workers. I had to make a snap judgment about the fire. Should we fight it? Evacuate? Wait it out? It only took a few milliseconds to make the decision. I called all the CMs over and told them we needed to evacuate to the outdoor patio, deputizing a few of them to go get other CMs in the nooks and crannies of our location, like order-take. I authorized someone else to go to the front of our line and shut the doors—I had just made the executive decision that the Café was now closed. Then I walked out to the On Stage side of our trayslide and called for attention among the Guests: "Ladies and gentlemen, excuse me, but we have an emergency and need you to leave the building right now. I know you are waiting for food, and I'm sorry for that, but there is no time. Please feel free to take whatever food or drink is on your trays now, with no need to pay, but we need to clear the line." No one asked questions, and rather than be upset by the inability to get all their items, many actually looked happy to get free food.

The assembled CMs behind me were tapped in quick succession to do other duties as they popped into my head, each a mere second after the last. I sent one person to close the Pastry Window in a similar fashion and another person to call the Café elevator and hold it via e-stop on our floor, so no one would use it. Another person was dispatched by foot to go to Club 33, whose dining room was directly above the Café and also would probably have to evacuate if the fire was not contained. Another person was dispatched to go downstairs, find our supervisors, and tell them what was happening. Still another person was sent to the phone to wait for the manager, who eventually did call back.

Very little time, maybe only two minutes, had elapsed since notifying the authorities of the fire. But managers from all kinds of departments had begun to appear, having sprinted from all corners of the park. A fire is a huge, huge deal. The radio "all-call," which I did not hear since we didn't wear radios, apparently said there was an electrical 904 at the Café Orleans, and the suits rushed in to help. They ended up evacuating even the outdoor patio, so there were no Guests left in our location at all. The fire marshal took longer to arrive, but he was there in a few more minutes. The smoke had not yet turned into flames, despite my fears, and by now even its tendrils had thinned out a bit.

The fire marshal took only minutes to figure out what happened. The Hatco warmer had insulation in the top of the unit, near the heating elements, and that insulation had somehow gotten too close, perhaps by someone jostling the machine. The insulation gave off a lot of smoke, but probably it didn't catch fire in the usual sense. So, in the end analysis, it was all smoke and no fire.

Had I overreacted? I didn't think of my actions as panic-driven (if anything, my mode of thought was cold and calculating, though admittedly rapid-fire), but I asked my manager on duty if my choices were right. He agreed the evacuation was fine, even closing the doors, and yes, even letting Guests go without paying for food. But apparently, I still should have waited for him to call before all that action. That's easy for him to say, in retrospect!

I felt comfortable about not having tried to fight the fire. We had fire extinguishers around, and I had been trained to use one. A few years back, the Leads had been gathered to undergo training on the extinguishers, and we were even permitted to use one, so that we could get the hang of it. But this fire had sent out a lot of smoke. I'd entertained visions of the entire wall of lacquered wood quickly engulfed in flames, and I knew that a single extinguisher would have had no chance in that event. Even after the investigation revealed no fire, implying my evacuation had been too cautious, and the manager told me I acted just a touch too rashly, I still felt that I could not in good conscience have acted otherwise. If there had been a fire in that exact spot, the entire building would have been engulfed, probably in just a few minutes. So I wasn't a hero and I didn't save any lives, but I took comfort in knowing that I could have.

Stupid Guest Tricks

Late-night talk show host David Letterman created the concept of "stupid pet tricks" that delighted his audience by showcasing animals' special abilities. I think of my stories of strange interactions with Guests as "stupid Guest tricks," partly because the "tricks" were often stupid and inconsequential, but also sometimes because the Guests themselves were stupid. CMs joked that Guests checked their brains at the gate. When they came to Disneyland, they sought to unwind and relax, which for some explicitly meant to stop thinking. Normally, CMs took that good-naturedly and considered interactions with inattentive Guests to be part of the job. The Guest was supposed to be allowed to turn off his brain; it's part of what he paid for with his admission ticket. But sometimes stupidity went beyond the usual inattentive behavior.

Here's an example. The Café had only one exit gate, and it was clearly marked. There was a twin of that gate on the other side, but it was for official use only, and it was labeled: "Please use exit on other side." At least a few times per hour, someone would nonetheless try to exit via this non-gate. It didn't push open, and it didn't seem to have an easy way to undo the latch, so most people gave up. The few who did not seemed to us CMs to be lacking a few brain cells, so often the CMs would let the next part unfold without interference. The Guest would reach into the latch and push it in directly to allow the gate to open. The quick spring, however, meant that the Guest always pinched his finger. The real way to open the gate safely is to depress a square button either above or below the latch. Years later, I still saw this kind of gate in heavy use at Disney parks. Why did some Cast Members let the Guest injure himself, albeit slightly? It was a kind of revenge on Guests in general, enjoyed as payback for all the other annoying Guests of the day. Besides, many reasoned, this particular Guest didn't seem to know how to heed the signs, and he deserved to be pinched for not following the rules.

Many instances of apparent Guest stupidity were really just moments of inattention. Often, this was Disneyland's fault indirectly. Since the park was so immersive and full of details, parents sometimes forget to watch children quite so closely, and temporarily lost children were common. There was a central office to coordinate the reuniting of parents and children, and when a CM encountered either side of the split party, she was supposed to call that central office, which then hoped to hear from the other side. We are also supposed to wander around the immediate vicinity with the lost party, hoping to reunite them on sight. As far as I know, rumors about kidnapped children being spirited out of Main Gate were patently false, but that didn't stop worried parents from becoming frantic and demanding that the gates be closed, the child be paged, and so on. Many blamed me personally for not closing Disneyland down for them, though we always found a happy reunion occurred after a few minutes. Early in my career, I was trying to calm down one mother and went to report the missing child, and I called Lost and Found by phone while the mother listened nearby. When she saw that I had called the wrong place—what we wanted was a different office called Lost Children (Lost and Found having to do with items, not people)—she sensed that I was new at this and understandably grew even more worried. Fortunately, even that child was quickly located.

As this story illustrates, I was not immune to the temporary stupidity that infected Guests—maybe the park itself was to blame after all. I was working in the order-take booth one day when a woman approached me and said she thought she had just been paged over the park-wide intercom system. The usual announcement was short and professional: "John Smith, please call the Disneyland operator. John Smith, please call the Disneyland operator." This woman thought her name had been invoked and wanted to know what it meant to call the Disneyland operator. I was uncharacteristically nonplussed and realized I had no idea, either. So I called a number I knew from being a Lead—Central Communications, the sub-department of Security that controlled all the radio announcements in the park and coordinated every major reaction. I asked how to get the Disneyland operator, thinking I'd have to dial a complex set of numbers. The person at the other end of the line was silent for a moment, presumably stunned at my idiocy. "You just dial zero," he said finally, pronouncing each word slowly. I consoled myself mentally, as I had considered that but rejected it because dialing zero usually reaches an operator from the telephone company, not Disneyland. It turns out Disneyland runs its own internal phones. Dialing 911 would have gotten me the Disneyland emergency team (in fact, those same folks at Central Communications). The Guest in front of me was eventually able to reach the Disneyland operator, where she ascertained that it hadn't been her name called after all. At least I learned something.

Nor was this my only moment of temporary insanity. Here's another one. When I was very new to the job, a girl about five years old asked her mother how big Disneyland was. Since I was standing nearby bussing a table, the mother passed the question on to me. "I'm not sure," I answered, "but for some reason, the number 42 square miles sticks in my head." Now, it turns out that that number is much closer to the size of Walt Disney World (and even then is incorrect), so at best one could say that I was mixing up my Disney parks. Disneyland at that time was more like 75 acres On Stage, with a 100-acre parking lot (the parking lot was bigger than the park!) Here's the punch line, though: the mother relayed my answer about 42 square miles back to the child, without thinking, and the child just let her eyes grow wide as if she understood. She had no hope of that. I was a seventeen-year-old kid at the time, so maybe my illogic could be forgiven, too. But this mother should have heard my answer and doubted me. Or maybe she did realize my mistake but was just being polite by not calling me on it.

Some Guests are inconsiderate, rather than idiotic. It was not uncommon for mothers to change their babies on the dining tables (particularly mean bussers would intentionally send those diapers down in the bustubs for the dishroom folks to dispose of, despite having trash cans around upstairs). Those parents may be used to their baby's various liquids and excretions, but I had to remind some of them that other people needed to eat on that surface. A fellow Lead named Steve once witnessed a four-year-old boy no longer wearing diapers grab hold of a lamppost out on our patio, and half-standing, half-squatting, strained loudly to complete a bowel movement right in his pants, while shocked patrons all around him tried their best to eat their lunch.

As a Lead, it's inevitable that one sometimes must adjudicate between people's personal beliefs. I once had a man come up to me and share conspiratorially that a woman was breast-feeding her baby on the patio. I nodded, not sure why he was telling me that, since mothers have a right, by law, to nurse pretty much anywhere they want. "And," he continued, "she's not even covering up. You can see a portion of her nipple every so often, as the baby detaches and reattaches." Apparently he wanted me to ask the woman to drape a blanket over the whole affair. I was being forced into making someone unhappy, either the man or the woman. I tried to steer a middle course by letting the woman know someone had noticed and requested she cover up. I did this as tactfully as I could, but it was still unbearably awkward. She gave me (politely but firmly) a simple answer: no. So I went back to the man, relayed her answer, and let him know I wasn't going to take this any further. The laws favored her side on this issue, I felt, and while I understood the man was acting on his beliefs, I couldn't impinge on someone else's rights in order to satisfy his beliefs. He snorted, and left the establishment shortly thereafter, dissatisfied.

Personal beliefs and toilet issues aside, not every complaint is rooted in Guest inconsiderateness. One woman called me over very tactfully, and in hushed tones so as not to alarm the rest of the dining patrons (she really was considerate), showed me the bright green living beetle that was nestled in the lettuce of her ham-and-turkey croissant sandwich. I nearly yelped aloud. She had narrowly missed taking a bite of it, she explained, and could she get her money back? I hastily refunded the entire party's cost of meals— Leads have wide latitude on this sort of thing—and apologized in about every way that I could. No one was hungry any more, and they weren't angry with us, so I could tell they weren't simply con artists out for a free meal.

The same could not be said for everyone. Most often a hair in the food was an honest mistake (we were required to wear hairnets and hats, but it was uphill work to get CMs to wear them correctly). Most often the Guest simply wanted another dish. It was when the Guest wanted a refund as well as another dish that things became more suspicious—especially if the hair in question was red, the Guest was red-headed, and none of the CMs had red hair. That happened from time to time.

By far the most common complaint, though, was about one particular menu item. The Club Dixie was really a puffed pastry with some bits of ham and cheese inside, but the menu was populated with themed names (the "Skipper's Catch" was

a tuna sandwich on honey wheat buns, for instance). We were
not allowed to just call it a puff pastry. Unfortunately, having
"club" in its title invited patrons to think of a club sandwich.
When they got to the sandwich window to pick up their
order, they were often quite annoyed. Other Guests paid for
it, disgruntled, and then returned for a refund and an
explanation. One math-challenged Guest complained about
the Club Dixie in that he didn't mind it not being a club
sandwich, but thought it didn't offer enough value. "I'd gladly
pay twice the price if only it were bigger," he explained to me.
I asked him if he would like to buy a second one. I didn't fully
understand this Guest. He wouldn't mind paying twice the
price for a pastry that was twice as large, but he resisted the
idea of paying for two of them at the real size. In retrospect, I
should not have applied pure logic to the situation. The Guest
didn't want to be made aware that he wasn't making any
sense. He wanted to be made happy. He didn't leave unhappy,
exactly, but I sense that he was somehow dissatisfied.

Over at the Veranda, a drink called the Mardi Gras Julep
caused similar headaches. The land was long famous for non-
alcoholic mint juleps, an invented concoction that detractors
thought had a sugary mouthwash flavor. These were sold at
the Mint Julep Bar, at the French Market, and at the Bayou.
Because the Mint Julep Bar looked to a casual observer like the
Veranda, patrons would swear they bought the mint julep
right there a few years ago, but it wasn't true. Their confusion
was aided by the menu, which advertised our drink as a Mardi
Gras Julep. It was really a red fruit punch. I petitioned for
years to have the name changed but never succeeded. Later it
became the Mardi Gras Punch, after a more sympathetic
manager moved in, and then finally simply Fruit Punch. I did
like the themed names somewhat; it's disappointing for Guests
to have no themed names at all. But there should be a balance;

the name shouldn't be misleading. The Mardi Gras Punch was a nice compromise.

The Veranda was the location where we'd see the most unusual mangling of our menu items, even apart from the julep confusion. I recall an achingly cute two year old who toddled up one day and drawled, "I want a critter" (meaning a fritter). But the most confusing was surely the man in his thirties who politely, if a bit absent-mindedly, asked for a congealed banana. Trying not to laugh, we eventually figured out that he was mis-reading the menu board, and wanted the frozen banana, which was listed as banana congélé (French for "frozen banana") on the menu.

Other Guest complaints came in the form of annoyance about our own CMs. Jonathan got many of these complaints. I've heard a few Leads confess they just tell the Guests "we'll be firing him soon" and that mollified the offended visitors. Personally, I never did that—what if it weren't true? That was especially risky as the 1990s progressed, and Disneyland began to heavily market annual passes, which increased the chance that repeat visitors would know the Lead was just lying to make the visitor happy, assuming incorrectly that they were tourists. Those frequent visitors quickly earned a negative reputation among CMs, since many had a false sense of entitlement. Derisive CMs named them "passholes" or "anal passholders." After a while, most CMs sensed that it was a small subset of entitled annual passholders who gave the much larger majority a bad name.

For whatever reason, I have several war stories associated with things falling out of the sky onto Guests. The most predictable one—bird droppings—did, of course, happen. Most visitors didn't complain when that occurred, since they realized our staff at the restaurant could do little to prevent it. But one woman demanded to see the Lead and exclaimed that her garment was quite expensive, and that Disneyland would need to pay for it. I couldn't placate her and had to escalate this complaint to my supervisor. When he came up, I learned something new: Costuming had laundry machines and could wash Guests' clothing in instances like this, and the Guest would be provided with a T-shirt from Main Street in the meantime (no doubt they'd get to keep the loaner shirt).

Birds caused a lot of trouble. At the French Market, where the menu included spaghetti, birds routinely mistook the noodles for worms and excitedly perched themselves atop chair backs while they pecked away. The problem was that that placed them directly over the chair seats, meaning they often left behind a minor mess. Bussers would need to check chair seats if they came to a table with leftover spaghetti and had to chase away birds. One man, disgusted with the bird droppings now on the backside of his pants, demanded that Disneyland kill all the birds. We couldn't poison them, I'd answer, since Disneyland is a bird sanctuary (which was quite true), which didn't endear me to him. On the other hand, no answer shy of a promised avian apocalypse would have made this bloodthirsty Guest happy.

Some enterprising bird was behind one of the most perplexing Guest complaints I ever saw at the Café. A female visitor demanded to see the Lead and proceeded to weave a wild tale of a costumed CM opening a window in the floor above the French Market and tossing a chicken bone at her. The woman wanted to know if the employee cafeteria was serving fried chicken that day (it was not, though the French Market served fried chicken all the time). The confusing part was why any CM would want to hurl gnawed bones at a Guest. Even more impossible: the area she was describing was the Cage, and those windows didn't open at all. Also, the bone was way too big to be a chicken bone. The woman stuck to her story. Finally, a woman from a nearby table beckoned me closer and told me she had seen it happen. The bone was not thrown by a CM; it was dropped by a bird who presumably was carrying it away to its nest. Once she pointed out the direction of the bird's path, I knew what had happened. The bird must have picked up part of a turkey leg, which in those days were only sold at the Big Thunder Ranch. That also explained the enormous size of the bone.

It wasn't only birds dropping things from the sky. The trees did it, too! One lady complained to me about the berry which had fallen from the tree overhead, but she had leapfrogged over "frustrated and irritated" straight to "irrational and abusive." As she explained to me what happened, she grabbed me by the shoulders, wheeled me about, and jabbed a finger into the back of my shoulder—hard—to illustrate what it felt like when the berry hit. She was worried not just about the blouse, but also the bruising. That didn't give her the right to essentially hit me, which is what she did, and she seemed to blame me personally. By this time I was armed with the knowledge that Disneyland can, in fact, launder Guests' clothing if need be, and I offered that to her. Of course, we also asked her to fill out a written statement of the event—one always has to think ahead to potential lawsuits. We had to fill out a statement form, which was really just a blank page with lines, every time there was some significant event. They were more common with CM-to-CM problems, but legal issues with the Guests warranted one as well.

The strangest object to fall from the sky was a gold woman's wristwatch, which cascaded down from the ether during a performance of Fantasmic! and hit some poor man on the head. He brought the watch to me and, because he was uninjured, he essentially shrugged it off, but he was curious to see if I could figure it out. I had a pretty good guess. Directly above the Café is the main dining room of Club 33, and I'd surmised that a Guest there had gone out onto the balcony to watch Fantasmic! The view from that balcony is better than ground level spots, and it would be quite good indeed, except for those aforementioned berry-dropping trees, which were partially in the way. I traveled up the Café elevator for a rare visit to Club 33 and was invited by the Lead there to head out to the balcony myself to find the person who had lost the watch. Normally this wouldn't be allowed, but a Restaurant Lead wears a business-style costume with a necktie, and I'd known to don my jacket before heading upstairs, so it was OK to be seen in the Club wearing this costume. I found several Guests on the patio still watching the show, and I easily located the woman who had lost it. She had no idea it had slipped off her wrist! She offered twenty dollars to the man who had returned it, so I headed back downstairs. When he demurred, I had to visit the lady upstairs one last time to let her know he had declined.

Without a doubt, the winner for Guest stupidity had to be the chowder fight which broke out on the Café patio. I didn't see it start. One of the cashiers came running up to me and told me there was a fight on the patio. I sprinted outside and called behind me to have someone phone Security right away. On the patio I saw people at two tables, sitting perhaps ten yards away from each other, flinging clam chowder back and forth.

One might think this was some harmless prank, or perhaps simply a fun food fight. But I knew better instinctively. Part of my job, after all, was to ensure that the cold food was kept cold enough (forty degrees) and that the hot food was kept hot enough (140-plus degrees) so that bacteria couldn't grow. I knew the soup was scalding hot. Besides, I could tell by all the angry screaming that this was not play.

The primary combatants were large men. I was perhaps 21 years old and pretty rail-thin. All I had on my side was my business suit-type costume. I did have one other attribute: a loud voice. "STOP IT!!" I commanded loudly and authoritatively. The trick to life-altering moments is to be decisive, never minding the hammering heart and dry throat. They actually stopped throwing things and paid attention to me. A little surprised, I turned to the cashier, who had followed me out, and I told her to make sure Security was on its way. Then I turned back to them and kept the peace. I even got the story out of them. Apparently it revolved around a girl at one of the tables and some lingering looks by someone at the other table. An angry word led to an exchange of insults and then an exchange of chowder.

Security arrived on the double. My guess is that they, too, had sprinted. The fight at this point was over, but all combatants were carted off to the Security office to talk it over and hash it out. Needless to say, the former fighters were not pleased. They glowered at each other (and at me) as they went away with Security.

The sad part was that this was a crowded day. There were innocent people sitting between those two tables, and they, too, were splattered by chowder. After the fighters had left with Security, I helped with the cleanup. This partly meant just mopping up the food everywhere, but mostly meant helping soothe over the Guests. Several onlookers in the vicinity had streaks of chowder in their hair. Many were upset, though not with us. A few demanded compensation for their meal costs, which, of course, we obliged.

Boys Will Be Boys

"Into every life a little rain must fall," intoned Jack Wagner, the Voice of Disneyland, on the rainy-day loop outside the ticket booths. This recording was meant to warn patrons that some rides might not operate if it rained that day. Even years later, the phrase echoed in my consciousness so much that it invited variations. In thinking about life at Disneyland, a variation of Jack Wagner's phrase comes to mind: "Into every workday a little play must fall." It wouldn't be Disneyland without some off-task goofing around, some of it tolerated by management more than others. This chapter is so named because it was simply true, at least at my restaurant, that it was the males who were much more likely to goof around, and who were especially prone to break the rules egregiously.

Verbal banter was all but a part of the job description. Anyone caught saying the wrong thing would be teased mercilessly. Poor Dwight mixed his metaphors with regularity. He once claimed a cake was so large that, "If you put those two tables together, it's about half that size," not realizing the tables were in fact the same size. Or his promised diet: "I'm going to be smaller than you and you put together!" (Uh, Dwight, you already are smaller than the two of us put together.)

The banter would turn playful at times. Dudley could never keep straight the name of our honeywheat buns and would instead ask for "wheat honeybuns." In the sexually-charged atmosphere of young Disneyland CMs, this quickly transmuted to something that sounded like admiration of the other person's buttocks: "I need wheat, honey buns." Something similar could be heard whenever a stocker would bring piping hot chowder or a heated entrée behind your field of vision. "Hot behind!" he'd call, so you'd know not to step backwards without looking, but the smart alecks would always reply with "Why, thank you!"

Poor Vanessa, who talked with too much "Valley Girl" slang, suffered for it when her audience took her words literally and lampooned the meaning. My favorite was the time she detected a bad odor and proclaimed, "I smell, like, a sewer or something." Dawson, ever quick on his feet, did not hesitate one iota. "Yeah, you do!"

CMs would carry the carefree and hormonally-charged attitude forward when they signed into the park as Guests. One particular rock formation, overhead while bobsleds navigate "Dolly's Drop" (so named for a CM who died on the job here, long ago), resembled the male anatomy when viewed from certain angles, so it became known as Penetration Rock. Even the company mascot was not off-limits. The statue of Walt and Mickey at the Central Plaza includes a three-dimensional nose for the famous mouse, who stood at Walt's waist height. CMs standing in a particular spot near the entrance to Frontierland could cause Mickey to hide almost completely behind Walt, with only his nose poking through the sideways view of Walt's waist, leading to the moniker "Walt's Little Friend."

Clearly, it was not a very politically correct society. Our manager Cathy once surveyed the array of pastries for sale and wanted more variety. So she commanded Steve, "Put some more color on the Serving Line!" Steve quickly joked to his pals, "Does she want me to put Linda out there?" The punch line was that Linda was African-American. Steve wasn't trying to be racist to Linda, who was popular. But the pursuit of verbal follies and puns was so relentless that many CMs did not hesitate to employ even racist jokes.

Words have meaning, of course, and sometimes they had real effects on the culture around them. One of our bussers,

Sam, was horribly slow at cleaning off tables. This annoyed the other bussers, because their workload was correspondingly increased, and Rudy coined the derisive label "four-to-one," since anybody could bus four tables in the time it took him to bus one. That became his name, at least behind his back.

Rudy, clever raconteur that he was, liked to combine concepts that normally didn't belong together. One day in the Veranda, for instance, he pondered what it would taste like if we mixed up the concept of a fritter and clam chowder. The fritter, as we told countless Guests who asked, was deep-fried batter rolled in sugar—a dessert. The clam chowder came served in a spherical sourdough bread bowl. Rudy wondered how it would taste if we sliced off the top of a fritter and used it as the bowl for chowder. He called it a "frowder" (the name "chitter" just sounded wrong), and it was deliciously disgusting among the Cast brave enough to try it.

Then there was Rupert, who loved to work as the Assembler, the person in the sandwich room who "assembled" the order before handing it to the Guest through the window. Rupert liked to interact with the Guests anyway, but he most often preferred to do it while saying something eccentric. "Welcome to Walt Disney's Enchanted Sandwich Room!" he might boom at them, but he wouldn't really allow the shtick to take over completely—he'd quickly get back to work and turn more serious. Still, that initial quirkiness would seem familiar to me when, years later, I met an Attractions CM named Maynard. Maynard always carried the act further and stayed in character longer, rather than just with his initial welcome.

Any CM who would misspeak would be mercilessly, though good-naturedly, mocked for days. An aspiring filmmaker, Sal never really had a way with words—for instance, he once forgot the word for "war" and could only come up with "gun...fight...thing." Sal was one day in the

Veranda, listening to Matthew describe how his current overtime pay was $20/hour, a dollar value that apparently impressed Sal. At that moment, a Guest walked up, and Sal turned to him to ask one of the usual questions, such as "May I help you?" What came out of his mouth instead was a mere, "Twenty?" Wires definitely got crossed there, and poor Sal was the subject of much ribbing.

Most playfulness fell into the realm of acceptability. When it rained, the storm drains in the street between the Café and the Bayou would overload, and a large puddle would form over one particular drain. I'd go out there, armed with a push broom, and deliberately eschewing a raincoat or plastic poncho, just so I could get soaking wet. I'd use the broom to move the water to another drain—one that worked well—and it was always tremendous fun. I think a good portion of the reason I liked to get soaked this way was that I was wearing the Lead costume—these weren't my own clothes.

Rain days were always fun at Disneyland, anyway. When CMs arrived at the Resort on rainy days, most tried to get rain gear issued to them from Costuming. Rain gear consisted of translucent slickers with hoods and was usually issued only to those folks who worked outdoors constantly, such as Security, Custodial, or Outdoor Vending. Otherwise, Costuming ran out of the rain gear—there wasn't enough to go around. Actually, they ran out each time it rained, anyway. Rain could sometimes be quite torrential, and New Orleans Square wasn't the only place to have trouble moving all the water out of the way. Coming in from Harbor House, CMs in some years would pass by a giant "softcover" pipeline. This was an emergency water pump runoff, from Main Street all the way Backstage to Harbor House, where it entered the sewer system directly. The temporary pump system became necessary after an early 90s flood on Main Street, when torrential rains far exceeded the drainage capacity of the Main Street sewers, and water flowed over the curbs and into the shops.

There was a rain plan at the Café, just as there was for most food locations. The normal indoor capacity was 12 tables and 34 chairs, but when it started raining, more tables were moved inside or bunched even closer under the awnings. The net result was a doubling of seats and tables inside, but at remarkably close quarters to one another. The French Market had an equally crazy rain plan: shut down one side of food service, and drag tables into this serving area. That got extremely hectic. The Blue Bayou, naturally, was unaffected by rain, as the entire operation was indoors.

Our cash cart provided a source of fun because it was so heavily weighed down by its metal box and the coins inside that one could stand on the back rod of the cart and find a perfect balance. This was most useful on the concrete downslope where the Backstage road passed under the train tracks, just behind City Hall. I'd be leaving work for the night and take this back road just so I could balance on the cash cart and coast down the road, building up quite a bit of speed. It was a lot of fun, and I never had a serious wipeout. In retrospect, though, a spill could have injured me pretty badly.

Once at Cash Control, I found that my night really hit its apex. There would usually be a line of cashiers waiting to turn in their funds, and most of them had only a single cash fund to turn in. As you might imagine, my presence was unpopular to people who got in line behind me, since I often had eight, or ten, or even twenty funds to turn in. So I began to go as fast as I could, and it didn't take too long before it evolved into a game.

The normal method for turning in a cash fund was fairly involved. I'd have to pull out the cash envelope and have the "whiz ticket" (on which was recorded how many $1 bills, $5 bills, and so on, were inside the envelope) that was stapled onto the envelope flipped open, facing the Cash Control attendant. Next to it I'd lay out a second whiz ticket, unattached to anything else, which specified the various coins

that were loose in the bag. The attendant would rip off the top two layers of the whiz ticket on the cash envelope (whiz tickets were filled out in triplicate), place those copies in two different stacks on his side of the counter, and then toss the fat cash envelope, still holding the bottom copy of the whiz ticket stapled to it, into a bin. Then he'd go through the same process for the standalone whiz ticket for the coins, placing his two copies into two stacks. This time,

the final copy would come back to me to stuff back into the bag, which had all the loose coins. Finally, I'd hand the bag to him, and he'd toss that into another bin.

It sounds like a lot of work, but when a CM did the same thing all day, he got fast at it. At Cash Control, Bernard was the fastest attendant (later, Bennie got good at it, too). Because I did this every night, I got fast, too, and eventually we began to "race." Whenever I'd have to wait on him, it meant he had messed up, and vice versa. We were well matched, and it went very fast. Eventually, the line behind me started to appreciate the show, and people would marvel at how fast Bernard and I were racing through fourteen funds (often, it took us about as long as a mere two funds for a typical cashier).

This attention encouraged me to raise the level of showmanship. I'd ask Bernard to leave the coin whiz ticket just out on the counter, instead of stuffing it under the coin bag. Usually he'd place it underneath something, because otherwise the air conditioning differential in the room would suck the lightweight paper out into the lobby, where I was. But I wanted that challenge. I wanted to pluck the whiz ticket out of the air and stuff it into its proper coin bag, because it was visually interesting for those watching. Often, I'd be off to the side of the counter somewhere, getting another fund ready to turn in (meaning I'd remove the cash envelope and the whiz tickets ahead of time, so Bernard could get started with it). That meant I'd sometimes have to lunge back to the window, where a whiz ticket was flying out into the lobby, and the whole thing became pretty kinetic. In a fit of pique one evening, when I was pretty far ahead in the race, I prepped the last bag and did a 360-degree spin on one heel (apparently I was channeling Michael Jackson), knowing the whiz ticket would be flying through the window as I did so. In one fluid motion, I ended my spin by catching the ticket on the fly, jammed it into the cash bag, reached through the window, and tossed it into the correct bin instead of letting Bernard do that part. It sounds insanely geeky now, but I swear that the crowd watching in the lobby actually applauded.

While these bits of playfulness may have still been "on task," there were plenty of times when the goofing off was more properly considered "off-task." In the sandwich room, there were lots of moments of downtime that needed to be filled somehow. Even in the busier moments, we could still engage our minds in games. So we evolved a movie game where we'd jump from movie to movie, connected only by a common actor—this was years before anyone popularized the similar game "Six Degrees of Kevin Bacon" (which proposed that any two actors could be linked to Kevin Bacon in six jumps, moving from one actor to another that shared movie projects). The hours would pass quickly when we played the movie game, or any of the multiple variations on the same concepts we evolved.

We veered more in the direction of horseplay with the games people played using the food. Tiny dressing cups could be used as basketball hoops for rolled-up pieces of bread. Or bread could be folded and twisted into interesting positions and then hardened by placing it in our bread steamer repeatedly. Dawson created bread dice in this fashion. Some of the bread creations were later hidden amid the props that lined the top of the sandwich room walls, which were there because the kitchen had a large window and Guests could peer in. We were doing all this stuff semi-On Stage.

Of course, the food's presence meant one had to fight the temptation to eat it. On my first day at work, my trainer Brad showed me how to waltz into the sandwich room, make a ham and turkey croissant sandwich, and stroll back out to the bus shack to eat it. I was way too terrified to mimic him (after all, that was stealing, a terminable offense). I once got caught popping a small snippet of Swiss cheese (really nothing more than a crumb left over after making a sandwich) into my mouth as supervisor Kellie rounded the corner. Be careful, she cautioned me, since that's stealing, technically. "For a little piece of cheese?!" I protested, and I was tormented by my friends with this tagline for years to come.

Many CMs seemed obsessed with eating the food. Dale was famous for taking our French rolls, adding butter and some other ingredients, steaming the thing until it was tremendously soft, and just eating it right there. Downstairs in the NOMK, chef Bobby affected a Southern drawl and sometimes rewarded his crew by whipping up biscuits for them to eat. "Hillbilly Biscuits," as he called them, became a staple after a while. Anton, working as a stocker, traveled up and down the Café elevator all day, and kept a spoon in his back pocket. In complete disdain for propriety (not to mention hygiene), he'd use this same spoon to dip into every pot of chowder he brought upstairs, and steal a bite.

CMs might let their attention wander when a particular job was boring or repetitive. One CM with too much time on his hands in the French Market noticed that the tile murals along the back wall contained scenes of antebellum Southern living which hewed a little too close to reality. All the African-Americans in the scene are engaged in physical labor, while all the white people are relaxing or watching over the African-Americans. These murals sat in plain view of the Guests!

Backstage, the tedium led to outright horseplay. In the dishroom, some guys dabbed mashed potatoes on tumblers and bus tubs, then stuck them upside down on the storage racks. These jokers once realized that the conveyor belt could be used to launch a small metal sauce cup, if the cup were placed in just the right spot where the belt crossed a dip in the table. Tom tried to mimic the success others had had with this tiny rocket, but bungled the attempt and instead broke the entire conveyor system.

Working Pastry Window often meant long hours with nothing to do at all, since the location was all but invisible to the Guests outside and was rarely busy. Many CMs wrote letters or notes, or even poems. Cell phones were rare in those days, and text messaging was non-existent. I once caught Hank constructing an elaborate structure made out of straws, filling much of the counter space and the significantly open area above his head.

Hank was involved in another prank that sticks out in memory. As closing Lead, I went downstairs to put the CM hours into the Employee Time Recording System (ETRS) computer program. All the CMs stayed upstairs cleaning their stations, and when I came back upstairs, the lights were all off and everyone was gone. This was highly annoying and irregular—they were supposed to have their work checked before they went home—but before I could get too far, everyone screamed "boo" and turned on the lights. They had been hiding, in places like inside the refrigerators. It had all been the brainchild of Hank and Dorothy.

In fact, Hank was notorious for finding ways to avoid working. I once sent him to work at the Blue Bayou, since they were understaffed that day and we had people to spare. This involved doing a costume change. Hank dutifully went back to the locker room, but rather than obtain a Bayou costume, he changed into his street clothes, slipped On Stage to the Starcade, and played video games for 45 minutes before finally returning to the locker to get a Bayou costume. I caught him slinking back into our area more than an hour late. The episode did reveal a crack in the system: no one was watching CMs as they were sent to do costume changes, and work avoidance became so common one almost had to expect it.

The grand opening of Mickey's Toontown provided Hank with one of his greatest "victories" in avoiding work. With a buddy, he simply walked around all night, not doing a single bit of work. Instead, he jumped on the trampolines set up for the event, took photos with the dancers, climbed up on the Fantasyland roofline, and wandered around inside Pinocchio's Daring Journey.

Then there was the Mouse-O-Rail. This was the front car of Big Red, the monorail car with a big bubble for the operator at the front. It had been retired from Disneyland long ago, but it had been recalled to be converted into a road-worthy car, designed to travel the country with Mickey and Friends as a way to promote Disneyland's 35th Anniversary. By this time, the Mouse-O-Rail was simply in storage in the back areas of the park. During a private party, several boys had been sent with the pickup truck to get tables from the back areas of the

park, and they ran across the Mouse-O-Rail. For reasons
known only to themselves, thought it would be funny to pee
on the Mouse-O-Rail. Nor was that the only peeing going on.
Dwight once apparently urinated in the Café elevator (there
was pretty clear evidence from folks in it right before him and
right after him that Dwight was to blame), but he denied it
consistently. Down in the CM bathrooms, DEC worker Trudy,
a new hire, was stymied by the fact that the only two toilets
were in use, so she squatted in the middle of the bathroom
floor and used the floor drain, where she was witnessed by
Vanessa.

The list goes on and on. In the elevator shaft, if one
stopped the car with the e-stop at the right moment and pried
open the doors, one would see an unprintable message about
yours truly scrawled in permanent marker. When working as
a busser in the Blue Bayou, Carson went to the bridge over the
attraction boats and dropped water on the Guests below. Dale
and Roy threw full Coca-Cola cans at Rudy and Dawson
during one private party, intentionally hitting the brick wall
behind them and sending spray all over them. Quentin and his
identical twin brother, Mitchell, who worked over in Critter
Country, impersonated each other sometimes for an entire
shift and didn't tell anyone. When we learned this years later,
it suddenly made sense that Quentin had inexplicably
forgotten how to do the most basic tasks in our operation.

Dale discovered that our phones, which did not dial out to
regular telephone numbers and only worked "in park,"
nevertheless could utilize a feature called a "tie line." Dialing a
short sequence could connect our "in park" phone to another
closed-loop phone at a different Disney property, so it would
be possible to call Walt Disney World toll-free, for instance.
Beaming, Dale demonstrated by looking up the tie-line
number for the Queen Mary (which was owned by Disney at
that time) and calling the engine room directly. "Engine

Room," came the quick answer on the other end. "Full steam ahead!" declared Dale with gusto. "Uh-huh," replied the man evenly, and then simply hung up. He must have heard that one before.

The managers' phones in the downstairs office were capable of dialing out, as was the phone in the Club 33 office. Hector, one of the Club 33 managers, was reportedly fired for making numerous long-distance calls to his home country of Turkey.

The New Orleans Square restaurants not only included telephones, they were also connected to each other by an antique intercom system. Some CMs found amusement in holding down all the buttons at once, so it rang everywhere and created a party line, with no one sure who was calling whom, or why. Tom and Hank took childish pleasure in using the phone and intercom systems to play pranks. Hank would sit in the downstairs office while on the phone with Tom, who was upstairs in the Café. Tom would buzz the NOMK's intercom, and whenever someone would approach the intercom to answer it, Hank would tell Tom, and Tom would hang up on the intercom, leaving the NOMK worker puzzled or annoyed. Repeated almost a dozen times, the prank definitely turned annoying!

On one's last day of work, it was not uncommon to play some kind of practical joke, in order to leave one's mark on the location. The most common prank was to go down to the Coke syrup room in Dry Storage, where the "bag-in-box" syrup was stored for the Café Orleans soda dispensers, and switch around all the lines, so that depressing the lever upstairs for Sprite might produce Diet Coke, and so on. Hank, on his last day, wanted to do something original, so he brought a dozen raw eggs to the Blue Bayou and hid them all over the place so well that they would never be found.

Eventually they turned rotten, and the smell wafted
everywhere.

While many of these instances of horseplay might have
landed one in trouble, there were a few instances where the
perpetrators got caught and indeed did get in trouble via a
written reprimand, skipping right over the verbal reprimand.
Rudy and Stan decided to arm wrestle on a stack of trays, and
Rudy unexpectedly broke his arm in the process—apparently
the combination of using his weaker left arm and standing at
an awkward angle was enough to snap the bone. Obviously
Rudy and Stan got "writtens," but so did Lead Steve, who had
been counting a cash drawer nearby at the table used for
sorting silverware and had done nothing to stop their
horseplay.

The Leads communicated with each other via a Lead Log,
a book with blank lined pages. At the end of each day, the
closing Lead would record new policies or new developments
that the other Leads would need to know, or would list out
specifics that the opening Lead the next morning might want
to pay attention to. Karl, Dawson, and Roy were three Leads
who took the idea one step further, and they began to use the
Lead Log to complain about their own CMs, often complete
with crude and inappropriate jokes, and to draw funny
pictures. Supervisor Tanya once picked up the log and added
an entry about a new policy she wanted everyone to know
about, and she happened to see other recent entries, which
prompted her to flip through it all. The Leads involved were
brought to the office, and it was communicated to them that
the Lead Log was a legal document, definitely not to be used
for this kind of shocking behavior. They all received written
reprimands on their records.

The Café was always locked in semi-friendly mortal
combat with the French Market for the same supply of shared
dishware, so a mostly-friendly rivalry sprung up over the

years. Hank took the battle to extremes, though, by calling the French Market's elevator up to the third floor, where the Club 33 had its storeroom, and loading it completely full of stuff they didn't need. Once he released the elevator, they'd be angry that it took so long, and angrier still when they saw it couldn't be used until it was emptied and the stuff returned!

No discussion of CM shenanigans is complete without mentioning one of the most common forms of Cast Member tomfoolery: sneaking around locations other than one's own. Robb bravely infiltrated the Matterhorn and took his picture next to the Abominable Snowman, and he explored the basketball hoop in a break area near the top of the mountain. For the record, it's not a full basketball court or even a half court, but there is some room to run around a bit. Robb also made it into closed attractions America Sings and Mission to Mars and wandered among the robotic performers.

Closer to our own location was Pirates of the Caribbean. Since the access doors to this location were right in our complex, and they were unlocked, the temptation was great to go explore. A great many people ventured into the treasure room, and many returned with baubles that were pretty cheaply built, once seen up close. I was always way too scared, since this seemed to be a terminable offense. That didn't stop others, however, and there was a great deal of exploring by intrepid CMs.

Those access doors also led to a catwalk above the Blue Bayou and the swamp portion of the Pirates of the Caribbean, where one could peer down upon the Guests below as the boats passed by. Having access from above meant all kinds of shenanigans occurred. Mean CMs might spit on them, or use a nearby Custodial hose to spray them. Hank waited for a boatload of loud kids to drift by, then threw a handful of pennies at the Blue Bayou tables as though the kids had been responsible. He felt bad, though, when the Blue Bayou Lead claimed to have seen the kids throw the pennies, and pursued the matter. The innocent kids ended up getting kicked out of the park that day.

Dennis once broke through the panels, and he would have fallen all the way down to the boats and the water, but fellow explorer Brian was right there and caught him before that happened. Amusingly, management thought the tiles broke by themselves, just due to age, and the next refurbishment of the Pirates/Bayou building included replacing ceiling tiles before others could "get old" and fall down on their own.

Brian was also once exploring the Haunted Mansion with Hank during operating hours. They opened one door a crack to peer On Stage, and by coincidence, the ride stopped at that moment. Panicked, they fled and got separated from each other. Hank made it to the ladder they'd started at, but Brian wandered about, and eventually got so lost that he resigned himself to being caught and fired. He did eventually re-unite with Hank without incident. This kind of excitement often incited, rather than dampened, further exploration.

Hank and Steve ventured out to the launching pad for the fireworks and settled into their golf cart to watch the show. Someone yelled at them to get indoors, however, and they had to leave the area. This was fortunate, as a mere three minutes into the show, a large shell exploded early and showered the area they had just vacated. Delighted by the close call, Hank tried to return another day with Brian, but was caught by area manager Jess, and reported to his own area manager.

Perhaps the grandest case of illegal exploration came from Geoffrey, who as an amateur rock climber longed to scale the Matterhorn. He befriended the official climbers, and traveled socially with them for some events in the local area, climbing terrain with enough dexterity to finally convince them he could handle the Matterhorn (which has a lot of handholds and footholds built into it, apparently, and is not a particularly challenging climb). So without anyone official knowing about it, Geoffrey geared up with the climbers, donned the same lederhosen outfit they wore, and simply ascended the mountain during one of their regularly scheduled climbs, in the middle of a crowded summer day. It was the view of a lifetime, he said, but I remained more in awe of the brazen nature of his illegal exploration. It happened right in front of everyone!

Raging Hormones

There's an old saying at Disneyland about the hormonally-charged environment. Here is the family-friendly paraphrase: "if you can't date someone at Disneyland, you can't date at all." Indeed, it was quite easy for even most of the shy folks to find someone at Disneyland.

As one might imagine, there were parties. Frequently. Working at Disneyland was a lot like being in high school, socially speaking. People looked for any excuse to drink, and they certainly needed no excuse to seek the company of the opposite sex. There was one major difference from high school, at least at my restaurant: the society was less fragmented into cliques at the Café than my high school had been. Everyone was welcome at these parties, and people were all more likely to be friends with each other. As noted at the beginning of this book, my timing and my work location may have been fortuitous, since other places at Disneyland did seem to have more cliques.

CMs hooking up with other CMs at these parties was almost a certainty. The parties often involved CMs from multiple locations in our department, and they occasionally turned wild. Christine, one attractive hostess from the Bayou, got really drunk and jumped up on a table, where she gyrated seductively as she removed layers of clothing. The rumor mill held that the folks over in the French Market partied *too* hard, using cocaine, whereas Café parties tended to be fueled only by alcohol. Of course, alcohol had its own ramifications. Stan, hung over and working alone in the Veranda one day, barely had time to make it to the trashcan before he threw up. The next time you see

Regardless of the party or the mitigating circumstance, there was some mystique about hooking up with someone from a location outside of one's own. It was more mysterious, certainly, and there's something to be said for not having to work on an ongoing basis with this person after the event. The latter scenario caused unending problems when two CMs who worked together learned to despise each other after a bad relationship, or even after a brief fling. Of course, the notion of seeing someone outside the department had limits. Bonnie, a vivacious girl in our restaurant, was actively stalked by a maintenance worker, and more than once she had to call Security to keep him away from her.

Most commonly, though, people found relationships from within their same locations. Once they became an item, one way to tell for sure was that they would store their paper timecards in the same slot at Harbor House, as if to imply an emotional union through the stacking of their timecards. Someone innocently browsing the timecards, looking for his own so he could clock in, might see the timecards of the two lovebirds together, and he would know of the relationship. Timecards for CMs under 18 were red, and they contrasted with the cream color for everyone else. It was a minor sensation when two timecards would be placed together that mixed up the colors, which meant that someone under 18 was dating someone over 18.

The dating and casual relationships were so common that most people at the location had kissed multiple others, and it entered my head to chart all of this by creating a "kissing web" that tracked who had kissed whom. The result was startling— it was a little scary to see just how interconnected the entire department was. Forget 'Six Degrees of Kevin Bacon'. One could jump from oneself to a mortal enemy in just a few moves on the kissing web.

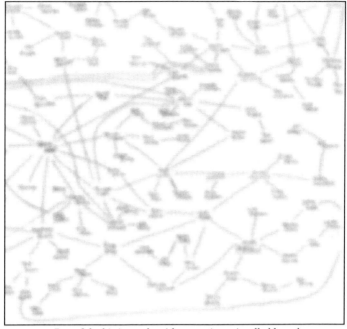

Part of the kissing web, with names intentionally blurred

All the smooching, of course, led to some marriages. I can think of seven marriages that resulted during my time there. But some of the relationships were a bit more risqué in nature than others. By this, I mean the managers and supervisors who would fall for an hourly CM. Area manager Joe was infamous for this. He wasn't in our area directly, but that didn't stop the whispers from spreading around the park. Closer to home was the hidden romance of Denver and Kathleen. Denver was an hourly CM, and Kathleen was one of our managers. Due to the power relationship, they hid their amorous connection from others, and it managed to last several months. Later, Kathleen married Jim, one of Denver's friends and another hourly CM. Human impulses are apparently quite hard to repress.

That includes the more base impulses. Kissing may not always have led to marriage, but it did often lead to sex, including sex right there in the workplace. Brad claimed to have had sex in the French Market elevator, and he was hardly alone in the boast. Tales of elevator sex were common, almost required.

One morning before opening, Dwight and Darla did the deed in the sandwich room, and Dwight wasted no time in telling everyone about it as they came in to work that day. A bit of blood on his apron, a by-product of the fact that his tryst with Darla came at an unfortunate time in her cycle, gave Dwight an idea. He faked slicing his finger with one of the knives used to cut sandwiches, and parlayed the spot of blood into a trip to First Aid. No one knows for sure that CMs really do go to First Aid, though, so it's possible that he simply wandered around for an hour, content to not be working.

Crossing a bridge from the Blue Bayou bussing floor, CMs could walk on the far side of the swamp and visit the shack containing the robotic old man in a rocking chair, visible to boats on Pirates of the Caribbean. Hank took incriminating photos of himself giving the Audio-Animatronics figure a lap dance, and performing oral sex on it. Speaking of oral sex, the shack was a popular place for it, since it was nominally hidden from view and semi-private.

The entire complex was so bursting with nooks and crannies that it was no surprise when people claimed to have sex all over the place. Anything slightly hidden had stories of sexual escapades attached to it: the Coke room, the Cage, and the so-called "cubby hole" in the French Market bus room, an alcove behind a sliding wall that led to an empty space underneath a staircase. The cubby hole sure seemed like a secluded spot, and a couple in here was unlikely to be discovered. You could peek through holes in the wood to see

On Stage, with Guests passing right next to you, and that merely increased the excitement of locations like these.

The Disneyland Ninjas

I had left New Orleans Restaurants behind in the late 90s, thinking my Disneyland career was over, but a couple of years later, my Café friend Dawson called and suggested I try to work for his new department, Entertainment Art (EntArt). A subset of the regular Entertainment department, this one did artwork, signs, banners, photo backdrops, floral arrangements, and displays for anything temporary in the park. Stuff that is meant to stay more permanently is done either by another Disneyland department or by WDI. EntArt thus mainly existed to provide décor for events, from press events to Grad Nites to private parties. I was hired to work on EntArt's crew. There was a cadre of artists who worked in our main building, and my primary job was to go install the artwork and decorations on the site itself.

EntArt crew was run by Ken, and the strength of Dawson's recommendation was all it took to get hired. There was no interview, really, and certainly no job skills test. I did have to go through Orientation again. This time it was in the Team Disney Anaheim administration building, and it was interesting to contrast it with my experience as a first-time new-hire. There was, for instance, less emphasis this time on pixie dust and the magic.

Ken walked me through the EntArt warehouse, which was located off-site but still very near Disneyland. Since it was on Olive Street, we simply referred to the building as "Olive." EntArt would later move from this building in 2007.

Ken showed me the four-truck fleet used to transport their props and equipment around. The warehouse was big, and it was stuffed to the gills with props. It was like walking through Disneyland history. This department had existed only since 1987—the same year that I started with Disneyland—so it was like walking through my own park history, with evidence of movie promotions and park-wide temporary themes in every nook. Dozens of oversized photo locations and backdrops were stowed down one aisle, signs aplenty stored down another aisle.

A typical day working for EntArt crew meant either setting up a location, or tearing it down (we used the Hollywood term, to "strike" the set). Sometimes we did both in a single shift, which meant lots of downtime in between. Actually, there was a lot of downtime anyway. Seldom were we rushed to complete a job, because when the job was first applied for, enough time was built in to avoid rushing, which was probably a good thing when we were prepping a stage for the press or the paying public. We'd set up temporary displays at the Disneyana convention or bring photo locations for Mother's Day to the Disneyland Hotel, or attach banners at Grad Nite, or stick signs onto podiums at press events. We were involved in premieres and park promotions like Super Soap Weekends and the Rockin' the Bay concert series. Often, at these same events, we'd bring along potted plants to arrange artfully nearby. Whenever red carpet needed to be laid down and taped in place, that was our job. The crew would be sent out with a salaried "designer" who was responsible for the overall event.

I was shocked at how much of the job revolved around signs hung up on freestanding poles and displayed around the Disneyland Resort. Because the square sign and the long pole resembled a certain candy, we called them lollipops. We were constantly dropping off or picking up lollipops around the parks. Once I knew to look for them, it became clear they were everywhere. It also illustrated just how much Disneyland and DCA were always in use for private and special events, as well as for temporary promotions.

Because we were often under stages or in dark corners, I wore a mini-flashlight on my belt. Since our jobs revolved around ropes and strings and attaching devices, I made daily use of a multitool that also hung on my belt. I started to feel like Batman sporting a utility belt. Maybe a better analogy would be to the military's special forces. To hang banners in hard-to-reach places, we were not only climbing ladders, we were also going over (or even under) fences, scrambling up to rooftops, or beating our way through foliage.

The best analogy of all, though, would be to call EntArt crew the Disneyland equivalent of ninjas. We didn't wear black (those are the "stage techs"), but our dark gray shirts helped us sink into the background just as well. One tremendous advantage of our generic costumes was that we

went everywhere. No place was off-limits, and no Backstage access was denied, if we needed to head there in pursuit of our goal. And like ninjas, it was our job to be invisible.

Costuming was handled simply. At our warehouse, we were issued several sets of branded polo shirts and cargo shorts, given a locker, and told that the soiled costumes would be picked up right there and fresh ones returned in their places. Guidelines for the Disney Look seemed to be a lot less stringent than in the parks. Indeed, the manager of the entire Entertainment department sported an earring, which was pretty far afield from the officially-allowed policy.

Scheduling-wise, we had one of the best deals in the whole park. We were B-status and had health benefits, but we weren't required to work every day. In fact, we only had to work when requested—but we were "on call" pretty much every day of the week. However, we could also turn down any particular gig, though few did, since of course we were paid only for the work we performed. Later, we were dropped to CR-status, but that was still a much better deal, with more flexible scheduling than just about any location in the park. Even better, for several months until the policy was eliminated, there were "paid ERs": if we finished early, and our shifts didn't require us to work up to the minimum four hours, they simply let us go home, and we got paid for the four hours anyway.

Occasionally I'd work a warehouse shift, putting away props and taking out new ones for the guys who were working the trucks to deploy. This required becoming certified in how to drive a forklift, a unique experience for me! Most crew shifts involved being in the warehouse briefly, anyway, to pick up the props for the day, and then to load them onto the trucks. Then the props had to be secured for transport, meaning I had to learn to tie knots. We used a simple square knot to tie rope to the stakes on the flatbed truck, then tied a tightened bowline to the prop to keep it in place (sometimes with two half-hitches in between to keep it really tight), and then we did the same thing with a second rope on the other side of the prop. The idea was that the thing had to be quite immobile for the journey to Disneyland on the public roads. Often we'd bring multiple props and décor on a single trip, so a good amount of time was simply spent loading the truck.

We'd really want the knots and ropes to be in solid working order. A prop that slipped could be damaged, and most of them cost thousands of dollars. Accidents were also possible. For the premiere of Haunted Mansion Holiday, a special dinner event was held inside the Blue Bayou, and we had crafted large sets themed to *Nightmare Before Christmas*.

I was transporting these flat wooden sets, aligned on a rolling cart, to the Bayou when the cursed cobblestones of Royal Street made my knot come loose, and the very heavy wooden pieces clattered to the ground, actually hitting one startled passer-by.

My memory of EntArt is dominated by many such mini-stories. This incident in New Orleans Square wasn't the only accident I witnessed. Early one morning, Jenner was driving one of the enclosed trucks near Avalon Cove, and he backed up right into a lamppost on the lagoon and knocked it right over. It was so incongruous-looking inside a Disney park to see such damage. They had it cleaned up before the park opened, but for several days the lamppost was clearly missing, with just a temporary cap on the wires in its place.

Those trucks took us all over, not just around the Disneyland Resort. We were dispatched to the El Capitan theater to set up the post-show areas, such as the large wooden flats holding aquariums for *Atlantis*. I worked a strike at Disney's Jungle Adventures, an ice-skating show at the L.A. Sports Arena which tried to combine *The Lion King*, *The Jungle Book*, and *Tarzan* into a single show. We had to strike the VIP room, which was heavy in netting and jungle designs.

But more often, we moved things around the Disneyland Resort. Once we were tasked with locating a shed behind the Disneyland Hotel. Atop it was an enormous eagle prop, clutching a globe below. It seemed oddly familiar to me. This sucker easily weighed 500 pounds, and it was not situated in a place where a forklift would have helped, so we had to muscle it across a makeshift bridge to another shed, and lower it from there. It was backbreaking work. We simply took the eagle, once down, back to the warehouse. Once home, I looked at old pictures to confirm my suspicion: this was indeed the Atlantic Richfield eagle prop that once stood atop the Autopia entrance in Tomorrowland. I had been manhandling history!

One time, in an event to honor the environmentally friendly policies (or "Environmentality," as Disney liked to call it) of a local school, I got to work the bird crew. This meant simply that I transported cages full of homing pigeons, donned a headset, and waited for the signal to let them fly. This event was being held in front of the Sun Icon at DCA, so I was camped out in the bushes, lying down and waiting for my chance to pull the handle and let the birds go. Josiah, my fellow bird crew member, later told me that he got all his birds out much faster by kicking the wooden baskets they were in and scaring them away, though one bird in his cage never flew at all. It could be that he injured it, though it's also possible it was a young bird not yet trained to fly.

We climbed buildings with abandon. I had to place a temporary sign atop the food facility at the Fantasyland Theatre—I still think of this place as Yumz, its original name, though at that moment it was called Troubadour Treats—and I got to crawl around up there. We had to hang a banner from what was then the ABC Soap Opera Bistro (later Playhouse Disney) in DCA, so that was another rooftop to my credit. To get out to the On Stage part of the roof, we had to shimmy on our stomachs under a fence.

It was customary to crawl around, atop, and under stages. We didn't set up the stages—another department of Stage Techs handled that—but we would decorate them. Occasionally, we'd work in them, too. For New Year's Eve in DCA, my job was to climb high atop a metal scaffolding and hide amidst the balloons. At the appointed time, I'd release the balloons and streamers to celebrate the new year. Normally the balloon release is done from a distance, but a Guest had pulled the ripcord early in the evening, and some balloons had trickled out, rendering the usual system inoperative for this party. I climbed up the tower to be ready to release them manually. The party in Hollywood Pictures

Backlot raged on, and eventually the live band counted down to zero, and I released the balloons to watch everyone party it up below me. And then came the park-wide announcement with Minnie Mouse ticking down the seconds. Oops! Apparently the band had jumped the gun a bit!

Working this job, I got to see plenty of new Backstage places I'd never seen before. For one thing, Disneyland was now a resort (DCA had opened just before my return), and since DCA was in heavy use, many of our events took us all around this new park. I became familiar with all the break areas and learned to view this park as a CM does—meaning one is always aware of the hidden Backstage areas, dumpsters, and offices behind building facades. The half-heartedly-named (and almost unthemed) DCA Café behind the farm exhibit was a frequent resting point for our excursions.

Of course, we didn't spend all of our time at DCA. We ventured out to the hotels quite often, and the hotel administration building came onto my radar. Called the Big Orange Building (or simply BOB), it housed yet another Cast cafeteria. It started to feel like I was eating my way around the Disneyland Resort.

Even at Disneyland itself, I made my way into new Backstage areas. I once prepped the "green room" at the Fantasyland Theatre for that night's Candlelight Procession host, David Ogden Stiers, spending at least an hour building a Christmas-tree structure out of a few dozen potted poinsettia plants and a metal frame. Absent this job, I never would have had reason to prowl behind the Fantasyland Theatre or Hyperion Theatre.

And I finally had a valid reason to explore the park and be in lots of new places, something I'd never had the guts to do "illegally" before. I visited the Indian village and walked the old mule trail in the hills of Frontierland. I was in the tunnels of Tomorrowland, and I dropped off scrap metal in the dumpster for metals next to Circle D Corral.

Or, intriguingly, I was inside attractions. That happened less often, but it did occur, and none was more vivid in my mind than the sanctioned walk-through I received of the Haunted Mansion, with the work lights on. I was bursting with excitement as we were led around, winding in and out of the Omnimover track and ducking through Backstage doors, climbing staircases and marveling at the maze of unpainted two-by-fours just behind any door visible On Stage. It was easy to see why being here alone could lead one to think the place was haunted.

In fact, our guide said she had had a creepy experience herself in the Mansion. One night, with just one other stage tech there, she was adding decorations to the chandelier in the foyer and re-stringing it. Whenever the two of them left the room and came back later, it was always slanted, as if too heavy on one side. They'd fix it, and it would be slanted again later on. This began to spook them, so they fixed it one more time and decided to actively watch it this time. For five minutes, they watched the chandelier and it did not slant. Then they left briefly, and when they came back in, it was again leaning to one side. They both decided to get out of there that evening!

Just what was she installing? The first-ever Haunted Mansion Holiday. This explained why I was given a walk-through. EntArt was the unit that designed and built the Haunted Mansion Holiday, a dramatic departure from using WDI for such alterations of Disneyland attractions. In those summer months of 2001, I worked several shifts as an "artisan" rather than on crew, and I helped craft many of the set decorations. The burned, black, four-pronged "sprays," like twisted wreaths, that hung in the Gallery between changing portraits, were done almost entirely by me. I'd start with artificial branches and twist them into the overall shape, and wind artificial wreaths through them that had been spray-painted black, then baked in an oven to melt and fuse them into that sinister burned look. Smaller twigs and berries were then added, each one individually twisted into place manually. We had done much the same decorations for regular round wreaths as well.

I was handed large swags made up of black feathers and told to glue occasional white feathers into place to provide a contrast. Our first attempts resulted in such a patchwork that when the designer tried it on, she said she felt like Cruella de Vil, so we used fewer white feathers after that. We also hung berries and twigs in these, but they were lost in the black feathers. Most of our work was for naught anyway. When these swags were installed in the banquet hall, hanging just in front of the large windows that looked down upon the translucent ghosts below, only the black feathers were visible in the dim light of the attraction.

For the queue, we took store-bought artificial pumpkins and added ivy strands and numerous branches with berries, stapling them all into place and giving the whole affair a more sinister look. They would later be placed atop columns at the perimeter fence for the Haunted Mansion.

Sprinkled throughout the attraction and in the queue were bowties done in the style of *Nightmare Before Christmas*: long black bows with white pinstripes, and shredded edges at the tails. A good many of these were crafted by me as well. This was done using simple black construction paper and a normal paintbrush that had bristles cut out of it at regular intervals, so that a normal brushstroke would produce white

pinstripes. The whole thing was later given a clear glaze and baked quickly to provide a sheen.

While I went crazy seeing white parallel lines, elsewhere in our warehouse the foam-core artists were putting the final touches on the large Jack Skellington face that would grace the Stretching Room. It was built in two halves, and I watched it take form a little bit more each day. The same was true of the large snake to be located in the attic.

That snake was to hold the "naughty and nice" list, and one day, our Lead, Cheryl, came around to collect the names of all of us artisans working on the project for the list. She asked us if we'd like to be listed as naughty or nice. The "Kevin" visible on that list, seventeen names down from the top, does indeed refer to me. Nothing made me prouder than to be a part, however small and essentially invisible, of the On Stage Show for Guests.

We didn't create the decorations for Small World Holiday, but we were involved in the ancillary operation on Small World Way, where enormous white wreaths with dozens of ornaments and hundreds of lights adorned the towers that lit the parade route. We had to manually re-string these wreaths every year and apply hot glue to install new ornaments. Of course, then someone had to hang the things.

As delighted as I was to be a part of the Haunted Mansion Holiday, the event that will stick the most in my memory is my workday on September 11, 2001. I had been scheduled to work a morning shift, but I knew of the attack on the World Trade Center and the Pentagon before I arrived at work. We were supposed to clean barricades at DCA, so they would be sparkling for the press event for Who Wants to be a Millionaire-Play It, scheduled to take place later that day. Disneyland and DCA never opened that September 11 as a precaution, but I desperately wanted to go shine up the barricades because I wanted to see the deserted daytime

Disneyland. I'm not sure why management agreed, but I got my wish, and we set off.

Security was highly tight—our truck was searched for bombs, even underneath, right from that first day—but they let us through. DCA was a complete ghost town; we saw one Security officer walking through Sun Court, and no one else. We scrubbed up the barricades and headed across the way to Disneyland, in our truck, and drove On Stage onto Main Street in broad daylight. It, too, was a ghost town and quite uncanny. We didn't see a single soul. It felt, for all the world, like a *Twilight Zone* episode.

We drove around Tomorrowland, marveled at the emptiness, went across to Frontierland and still encountered no one, and finally made it up to the Haunted Mansion (in those days undergoing installation of the first Haunted Mansion Holiday) to check on something that was supposed to have been delivered. For that entire time, we didn't encounter any people. Everyone must have been called off and told to stay home on September 11.

I had seen Disneyland empty of all people on many occasions, but it was always at night. It was interesting, in a clinical sort of way, to walk back from my location long after all the Guests and even the workers had gone home, to see the lands illuminated by powerful floodlights so that third-shift custodial workers could do their jobs. The highly themed attractions and environments looked somehow naked in that artificial light. It was much more fun to walk back during that "sweet spot" between the clearing of all the Guests and the commencement of third-shift activity. If you managed to time things right, you saw an empty Disneyland with the regular Show fully intact: twinkle lights glittering on the trees in the Central Plaza, area music blaring from Main Street, regular (muted) lighting resulting in a darkened streetscape, and a blanket of oblivion and timelessness draped over the carefully orchestrated artificial reality of the themed environments. That was always, in a word, magical. Even veteran CMs would gape at the magnetism of Walt's park, experienced as few had ever seen it. But whereas a deserted Disneyland at night sparkled with charm, the deserted Disneyland during the daytime on September 11 generated an uncanny feeling. Sigmund Freud defined "uncanny" as that which is familiar-yet-foreign at the same time, a feeling of home/not-home that makes us uncomfortable. I found the empty Disneyland on September 11 to be uncanny. That haunting moment—America's park designed for the public (and usually teeming with masses) suddenly denied any human presence at all—will stay with me forever.

After about a year of working for Entertainment Art, opportunities on the East coast beckoned, and I bid Disneyland adieu once more, this time for good. My tenure in the Entertainment department had been much shorter than my time in New Orleans Restaurants, but the experiences were more varied and more sharply personal. I'd touched Disneyland history here, which made the experiences just as unforgettable as those fun times and fast friends in New Orleans Square.

Escaping the Mouse Trap

When people leave a location after working there for only a few years, there are seldom any send-offs. That was true of my time in EntArt. But when they had been there a decade or more, it was customary to commemorate the occasion somehow. Regular CMs were often treated to a gift that had been bought by other hourly CMs, who each chipped in a few dollars. One common gift in our area was a personalized glass mug from the nearby Arribas Brothers glass store. My friend Rudy, after more than ten years, was treated to the mug and a hardcover Disneyland souvenir book that we all signed like a high school yearbook (complete with raunchy messages and images from Elon, one of the more artistic CMs). We wanted to buy him an engraved medallion from the Pieces of Eight store. The mechanical device used a lever to move through the alphabet, and if we messed up, the effort was ruined. As a result, poor Rudy got a souvenir that tried to be ironic but ended up unintentionally funny due to the typo in its inscription: "I worked here for ten years and shis is all I got."

My own departure after a decade included the mug and some other gifts, as well as a poster from management, dominated by Mickey Mouse looking back over his shoulder and giving a wave. Across the top was always a message such as "so long." Mine said "Auf Wiedersehen" because I spoke German. People used these posters to scrawl messages of friendship and farewell.

Downstairs in the supervisor's office, I had my exit interview, a customary event used to chronicle and track people's reasons for leaving, and then there was a party. The managers had bought me a cake. While that was not too unusual— others had had one, too—mine was decorated in honor of my precision with operating hours, labor percentages, and "sales per labor hour" (SPLH) calculations: drawn on the surface of the cake in colored frosting was an Ops sheet!

Big, expansive good-byes were also unfortunately part of life when a current (or very recent) CM died suddenly. New Orleans Restaurants included several hundred people—it was a big department—and a good chunk of them came out for a funeral of a fellow worker. That happened for a guy in the Blue Bayou, and also for one of our own at the Café Orleans, shortly after his tenure at Disneyland.

Shy of an early death, though, most of us ex-Disneylanders found ourselves in a fairly tight circle. Many of us have kept the friends we made at the park. And a subset of us hired back into the park again and again. Every time we thought we could get out, we got pulled back in again, lured by the magic, or the friends, or the dream itself.

In a way, there was no closure, and none was possible. Being caught in the "mouse trap" is permanent. But that's a good thing. If the mouse trap is a cage, at least it's one that embraces fun, fantasy, and escapism: one lined with memories of good times and youth. You can take the Disneylander from Disneyland, but you cannot remove the Disneyland still inside every ex-Disneylander. The park changes everybody.

Most of us who worked at Disneyland for an extended time look back with fondness at our years working in the mouse trap. This nostalgia is part and parcel of what Disneyland stands for in general. Think about Walt's park when it first opened: a large chunk of it celebrated nostalgia for bygone times. To be nostalgic is, in a very real sense, to experience what Disneyland does to each visitor.

Other Disneyland CMs are just as nostalgic as I am for their versions of Disneyland. My stories may be specific to me, but they are hardly unique in the wider sweep of the Disneyland Cast Member experience. There are thousands of CMs and former CMs who have more interesting anecdotes than I do, and I hope this book inspires them to record their stories as well. Disneyland is not just my mouse trap. It's the device that traps all of us, Cast Members and Guests alike, and wraps us up completely, immersing us in its magic. I'd call that mouse trap "home" any time.

Glossary

ADO – Authorized Day Off. Usually, ADOs were requested in advance and noted on the published work schedule. ADOs could be part of the regular two days off per week, or a third day (though this was more rarely granted). The term was also invoked when someone was called at home before a scheduled shift and offered the day off, since the park was less busy than had been planned for, and too many people had been scheduled.

Area manager – used to be responsible for an entire land, with all business divisions in the area reporting to him.

Area supervisor – the immediate boss for location supervisors who divide up a department of intelligently grouped locations. The area supervisors, in turn, reported to the area manager. In later years all supervisors and area supervisors had been converted to managers and assistant managers—the same idea, but smaller "business units" than a department.

CM – Cast member; company lingo for "employee."

Code V – radio-speak for announcing a "protein spill" (no one wanted to say vomit on the open airwaves) that would need to be cleaned up. Often, the mess was covered by a scented sawdust concoction commonly known as "pixie dust," which absorbed the liquid and made it easy to sweep up.

CR – short for "casual regular" and often simply called "C" status; an hourly employee who works weekends year-round and five days a week during all school holiday periods (including summer and Christmas break).

CT – a part-time hourly employee who works five days a week during all school holiday periods (including summer and Christmas break). CTs had no seniority, so shifts worked were usually quite short.

DEC – Disneyland Employee Cafeteria. This eatery, deep underground in New Orleans Square, began as the Racing Pit, turned into the DEC, and still later become the Westside Diner.

DM1 – Duty Manager-1, or the person in charge of all of Disneyland operations at that exact minute. This position was held by a rotating crop of area managers and area supervisors. Before the mid-90s, it was called Ops-1.

Disney University – internal classes to train and professionally develop Disney's CMs. Instructors were seasoned hourly and salaried CMs.

Double-Back – By contract, CMs were allowed nine hours between shifts. Any time spent working until that nine-hour threshold was reached had to be paid at double the normal hourly rate. Regular overtime was only 1.5 times the standard rate of pay.

Double-Time – CMs were paid overtime for shifts that lasted longer than eight hours. After twelve hours, however, the pay rate shifted to twice the normal pay rate.

Empowerment Evolution – The 1995 attempt by then-new park management to introduce modern accountability and market forces into older Disneyland methodology and power hierarchies. The name was meant to "empower" rank and file employees by removing the need for their management to make all their decisions for them.

ER – Early Release; the permission to go home before the scheduled end of one's shift. CMs were only paid until their revised shift end, but ERs were popular, since a good many CMs wanted to work as few hours as possible, not the maximum.

ETRS – Employee Time Recording System; a computer program. This was Disneyland's first computerized system to track employee labor hours. Previously, paper timecards with time clock stamps and handwriting in ink provided the only means of tracking employee labor hours.

Guest – Disney term for customer.

Harbor House – the entry point to Backstage and the time clock shack that marked the beginning and end point of a CM's day.

No Strings Attached – a CM program for making a dissatisfied Guest happy. Hourly CMs were empowered to replace food or merchandise without undue paperwork, or in some cases to offer freebies just to rectify a situation.

RFT – short for "regular full time" and often simply called "A" status; a full-time hourly employee.

RPT – short for "regular part time" and often simply called "B" status; an hourly employee five days a week but usually not quite 40 hours.

SAM-1 – Security Area Manager, or the person in charge of all of Disneyland's security operations at that moment.

SPLH – Sales Per Labor Hour. Together with "labor percentage of sales," this metric was used to define how efficiently a shop or restaurant was being run. The calculation simply expressed how much money each man-hour of labor was producing, on average.

Supervisor – the lowest-ranking member of management. These salaried individuals worked under an area manager and jointly oversaw all the locations of a large department. In the mid-90s, they were renamed to "managers" and "assistant managers" and made responsible for individual locations rather than sharing responsibility for the many locations of a larger department.

TDA – Team Disney Anaheim; the name of the on-site administration building.

TPO – Theme Park Operations; the division of the Disneyland hierarchy that actually works in the theme park itself.

Walking Time – fifteen minutes (in later years, changed to twenty minutes) granted at the end of one's shift to leave the location early, walk back to the lockers, and exchange a soiled costume for a clean one to be used at the next shift. Disneyland emphasized the expectation of a clean costume by paying for the time needed to change it out daily.

About the Author

Kevin Yee, a Disney fan from birth, spent more than a decade working at Disneyland and cultivating a never-ending fascination with that park's rich traditions and history. Now relocated to Orlando, Kevin enjoys the Disney offerings on both sides of the country.

Kevin is the author of several Disney books:

- *Tokyo Disney Made Easy*: This guide to Tokyo Disneyland and Tokyo DisneySea takes all the guesswork out of a journey to Japan and the phenomenal Disney parks there. You'll have step by step guidelines for what to do and what to expect, so there is no worry whatsoever on your visit, even if you don't speak a word of Japanese.
- *Walt Disney World Hidden History*: Hidden history and insider tributes at the world's premiere theme parks and vacation destination. Locate the homages and scraps of information scattered about the parks, and soak up the details that make Disney unique.
- *101 Things You Never Knew About Disneyland*: Hidden history and insider tributes abound at Disneyland, and this book charts all of them, to make your visit to Disneyland all the more magical by reveling in the history all around you.
- *Magic Quizdom*: A trivia book dedicated only to Disneyland, this book specializes in historical items and dates for Walt's original Magic Kingdom.

An online journalist and columnist since 1997, Kevin now publishes at MiceAge.com and UltimateOrlando.com.

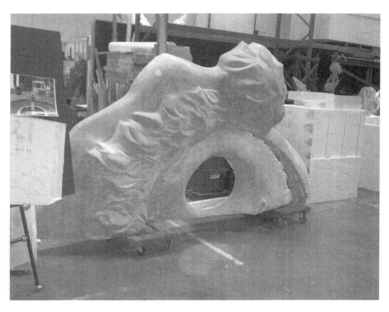

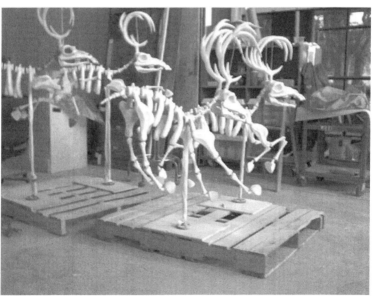